With ve
wi...

Ri alexande

That's Life Kid

Enjoy!

Our house in the Lake District

That's Life Kid

DI ALEXANDER

A Memoir

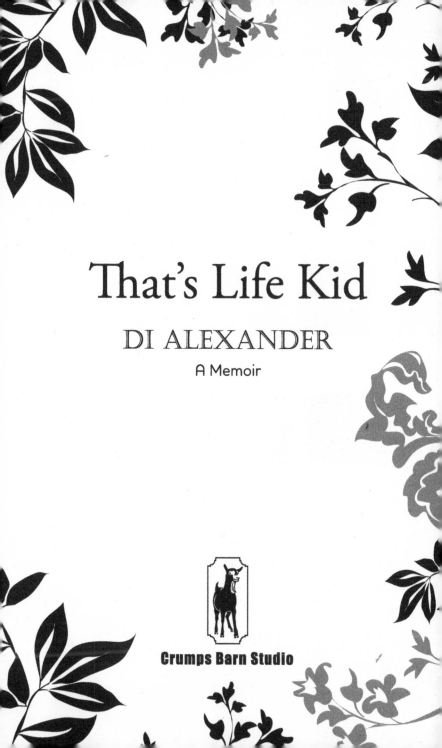

Crumps Barn Studio

Crumps Barn Studio
Crumps Barn, Syde, Cheltenham GL53 9PN
www.crumpsbarnstudio.co.uk

ISBN 978-1-8382298-0-1

For my family, whose love and humour made being a kid such a happy time and such fun for me, and especially for Martin who died just before this book was published

*On the terrace with Mum at Oliver Close, the
house we lived in with my grandparents*

Chapter 1

THE STRANGER

Christmas 1945. I was three years old and I was sitting at the bottom of the stairs in my grandparents' old slate house in the Lake District, wondering however I was going to manage to wait another two days until the Big Day. I was too young to remember other Christmases but I knew that this one was going to be like no other – and not just for me.

The war had ended, the austerity of the post-war period had not yet kicked in and the people of England were set to celebrate as never before.

'Hello, chum,' said the stranger as he came through the front door.

I remember thinking it a bit odd that he called me by the nickname only used by my immediate family. However, he looked nice and friendly, and talking to him would pass a few more minutes of that time I had to get through before the joys of Christmas morning.

I was pretty talkative even then – nothing new there – and as an only child who was used to conversing mainly with adults, my vocabulary was wider than that of most three year olds.

'I'm just so excited,' I burst out, 'because this is going to be the best Christmas ever. I'm hoping for a dolls' house. It used to belong to a friend of my Mummy's. They're rather scarce because of the war, you know.' – No flies on me even then – 'And my auntie and uncle, my two cousins and my other granny are all coming to stay.'

I added without even drawing a breath, 'And, best of all, we hope, we so hope that my Daddy will be home from the war. I've never met him because he's been a prisoner since I was born but now he's free and he's on his way back. He'll have to be quick, though, if he's going to be here in time for Christmas Day …'

My grandmother, who was making mince pies in the kitchen, must have heard my excited voice, and came to see what was going on. When she saw the stranger she ran towards him and hugged him, not even pausing to wipe her floury hands.

'Oh, Geoff! You made it, we were so afraid you wouldn't get here in time! And I see you two have met already.' And turning to me she said, 'Well, Chummy, what do you think of your Daddy?'

Then the stranger picked me up and hugged me as if he would never let me go.

Daddy in his uniform before he left to join his regiment, the Royal Army Medical Corps. I would meet him for the first time six years later

Chapter 2

CHRISTMAS 1945

That year was a Christmas to remember. It must have been, because my memories are so clear even after more than seventy years.

The next day, Daddy and I walked hand in hand to the little wood which adjoined our garden and he cut down a magnificent Christmas tree which we dragged home and put up in our hall. I don't suppose it was particularly magnificent but it seemed so to a three year-old.

We weren't stealing it, by the way; the wood belonged to us. Daddy, who was always up to mischief, especially after four years of German-baiting in prisoner of war camp, thought it was a bit soon to be leading me into wicked ways.

The tree stood bare-branched until Christmas Eve when, according to Mummy, the fairies would come and decorate it. Actually, I think it was a ploy on her part to have a nicely decorated tree and not one that had all the decorations in a big mass, just as high as a small child could reach. I wished I'd remembered about the fairies when I had children of my own ...

On Christmas Eve the rest of the family arrived – Nana, who was Daddy's mummy, Uncle Joey and Auntie Stella and my cousins, Hilary and Martin. Hilary was older than me but Martin was just a baby. He sat happily on the floor and smiled at everybody. I didn't know at the time, but we were to be boon companions all our lives, sharing joys and sorrows – and many more Christmasses.

Two very excited little girls went to bed that night, having first left out a large glass of creamy milk and a homemade minced pie for Father Christmas. I must have gone to sleep pretty quickly because the next thing I remember was waking up the next morning to see a dolls' house which stood resplendent in a corner of my bedroom. My mother had many talents but wrapping up parcels wasn't one of them and the dolls' house had really defeated her.

So there it was, with its mock Tudor woodwork, its painted green creeper and its red tiled roof. It had tiny windows which opened and shut and you could open the whole of the front and see the rooms inside, complete with tiny pieces of furniture and a family of dolls made,

I think, of wire and felt, and beautifully dressed. I can remember Mummy Doll's blue suit to this day. Even better – it had electric lighting which worked from a battery in the garage. I was entranced and it must have taken a lot of persuasion to get me to dress, have breakfast and go to church.

We walked to the little Italian style church on the other side of the river which ran through our garden and which in those days was the boundary between the counties of Westmoreland and Lancashire, crossing the wooden bridge which the floods of 1947 were to sweep away.

The vicar was an elderly man, serving out his time. Most clergy were old then as any young ones had been serving abroad during the war.

I was bored out of my mind as he droned on and on and in the end I could bear it no longer. I stood up on the pew, turned round and said in ringing tones to the assembled congregation, 'I do wish he'd hurry up. I got a new dolls' house for Christmas and I can't wait to get home to spring clean it.'

What came over me I really don't know, I was generally a polite child and rude behaviour would never have been tolerated in our family. What was even stranger was that, although we made a hasty exit, I never really got into trouble. I think the whole family was delighted to get out and get home …

While the lunch was being prepared, Nana found me a nearly empty bottle of Johnson's Furniture Polish and I set to work. I can smell the polish to this day. I couldn't tell if the doll family were pleased with my efforts – they didn't smile much – but I was. And that dolls' house gave me hours and hours of pleasure before it was eventually passed on to my little cousin Claire.

Christmas lunch cooked by both the grannies was amazing. After all the privations of war they had managed to procure a turkey (I suspect from kind Mrs Stables from the farm up the road who also supplied us with lots of butter and cream – all illegal in that time of severe rationing). They'd also found the ingredients for a Christmas pudding, minced pies and all sorts of other Christmas fare.

Grandpa, who adored Christmas as much as us children, carved the turkey and we filled our plates with vegetables and Granny Bradshaw's legendary gravy.

The pudding was rich and very sweet (where had Granny got all that sugar from? She must have been saving the coupons for weeks). We all loved it but it proved a step too far for my father, so recently released from prisoner of war camp who had to rush away and be sick. Poor Daddy – this happened so many times in the months which followed.

After a vain attempt to persuade the children to have an afternoon nap (mainly because the grown-ups wanted one), we all sang carols round the piano which Auntie Stella and Grandpa, who were the musical members of the family, took it in turns to play. Whenever it was Grandpa's turn he sat me on his knee with one arm either side and I watched as his stubby fingers ran dexterously over the keys – he didn't have traditional pianist's hands at all – and we all roared out the age old carols.

The rest of the day is a bit hazy. I think Hilary and I were so tired after all the excitement that we were put to bed early and were soon asleep, me clutching my beloved Pooh Bear as I was to do for so many nights of my childhood.

What a Christmas it had been! I have celebrated many Christmases since – many more lavish than this one – and enjoyed them all. We were too young to realise it, but for the adults it was the first Christmas of joy and hope for seven dreary and frightening years.

"Peace on earth – good will towards men!"

At last.

Chapter 3

DADDY

We had a lot of fun, my daddy and I, during those first few months after he came home from being a prisoner of war. He could make almost anything out of wood, using skills he had learned as a boy and honed in the camps, whenever he was able.

That first winter, he made me a sledge and pulled me over the snow covered lawn and along the frozen river bank. And as winter gave way to spring, he fixed up a fine wooden swing hung by thick ropes from one of the twin larch trees at the bottom of our garden.

I still have a photograph of a laughing, blond haired little girl, swinging among the trees. I was wearing a green coat – I know it was green, even though the photo is black and white, because I remember my granny making it for me at a time when children's clothes were hard to find. I loved that coat.

In the summer he made me a child-sized wheelbarrow.

I didn't do much gardening with it (gardening wasn't my favourite pastime then, and it still isn't), but I pushed it round filled with my favourite toys, including Pooh Bear who went with me everywhere.

Then he showed me how to make a strange little toy which he had first made as a prisoner. It was formed from an empty cotton reel, some matchsticks and a rubber band, and when you tightened the rubber band and set it going, it moved along on its own. I was fascinated and we got through a lot of rubber bands …

Daddy had bought into a partnership with a much older doctor and their surgery was in Ambleside, the nearest town. Dr Johnson had a bushy white beard and wore a three piece suit with a watch and chain. He must have been relieved to hand over a lot of his work to his energetic new partner – even if Daddy did dress a bit shambolically in a creased college blazer and shabby grey flannel trousers and, for formality's sake, wore a tie which had definitely seen better days.

He was much in demand, though, because his skills as a doctor were quickly recognised among the many patients in this sprawling Lakeland practice. Being a country GP was just where he wanted to be – and at such a time of change as the NHS came into being.

Much later in life he told me how he had been

promoted to the rank of major towards the end of the war and we giggled about the numerous men who still used their military titles long after the war was over. 'It's a doctor that I'm proud to be, not a bloody major,' he said.

Sometimes he would take me on his rounds and I remember one very wet day in early spring when we drove slowly along one of those narrow, sunken lanes that are so much a part of the Lake District. He said to me, 'Whatever you do, chum, don't open your door.'

I had no intention of doing so but I was curious to find out the reason so I stood up in my seat in his old Wolsley – no seat belts then – and looked out of the window. Water was lapping half way up the door!

But he drove on until we come out of the flood, completely unscathed. That was my daddy all over. He would rise to any challenge and the worse the conditions, the more he revelled in them.

He became the doctor who went out with the rescue teams to take injured climbers down from the mountains, he was doctor on duty during the Lake Windermere swim and various attempts at the water speed record. Wherever there was danger or risk, it was Doc Lancaster who was called upon – often in the middle of the night and in appalling weather. He loved it.

He did take time off to play rugby on Saturday

afternoons and there too, needless to say, he was always in the thick of the action. He always came home covered in mud from head to toe.

My mother refused point blank to scrub his rugby kit as we had no washing machine, or even a boiler. But, as ever, he had the answer.

He tied his muddy kit in a bundle with a thick rope, attached the other end of the rope to a rock on the river bank (the river, if you remember, ran through our garden), and threw the clothes into the water as far as they would go.

There they stayed until the following Friday when he rescued them, squeezed them out and draped them over the ancient coke boiler, known as 'the donkey', in the cellar. They never looked quite clean and remained rather creased but as he wasn't into sartorial elegance he didn't care.

As the year wore on it became obvious, even to me, that all was not well with my parents' marriage. Sometimes, after I had gone to bed I would hear raised voices and would creep out onto the landing to hear them in the middle of a row. It was very unsettling for a child like me who had never really heard anyone raise their voice in anger.

I've often thought since what it must be like for

children in really violent households to hear that sort of thing - and much worse – going on night after night.

Looking back, I realise that my parents' marriage never really stood a chance. No one else was involved – the only third party was the war. When they married they were both twenty one, my father qualified and immediately signed up for the Royal Army Medical Corps.

I remember my mother saying how put out she had been by his eagerness to go to war but that was how he was – full of enthusiasm for whatever excitement was next.

After he was posted to North Africa they hardly saw one another, although he must have been home on leave sometime in the early autumn of 1941 or I wouldn't be writing this now …

They were very young and by the time they were a little older they were used to leading separate lives. It was never going to work.

Of course, a lot of wartime marriages did survive and there was very little divorce but I often wonder how well these marriages worked after the war was over. I consider myself very lucky that I was not subjected to interminable quarrelling and that in the end I had a loving relationship with both my parents and the bonus of a wonderful stepfather who became my best friend.

At the time, though, I was heartbroken to see daddy

drive off in the old Wolsley with his luggage piled up and his bicycle tied to the back.

Daddy went to live in the flat over the surgery and, except when he came back briefly to collect the rest of his possessions, I didn't see him again until I was 13. This seems incredible in this age of regular access or even joint custody but it wasn't the case in 1946.

I should report here that I was traumatised and that it scarred me for life, but it wouldn't be true. I was four years old and I loved my daddy but children are very resilient and I was still surrounded by a loving family and a way of life that was familiar. I missed him a lot but I sort of accepted that this was how things were. Children did in those days – we'd been apart an awful lot already, after all.

*Meeting Daddy for the first
time in 12 years*

With my wheelbarrow made by Daddy,
full of toys

Mum during the war. Wherever did she get those trendy shoes?

Chapter 4

MY MUM

My mother was greatly loved, and not only by me. She had the gift of inspiring love in everyone she met – her family, her friends, my friends, our cleaning lady, the window cleaner. Even the people who served her in shops loved her, and the traffic warden who, if he saw her looking for a parking place, would stand in the nearest slot until she could get to it.

She always used to say that she had never passed an exam in her life but this didn't mean she wasn't intelligent. It was she who taught me a love of poetry and literature, who took me to the theatre, the cinema and art galleries but who also wasn't too snooty to take me and my cousins to the illuminations, the Tower Circus, the glitzy pantomime and the end-of-the-pier shows in nearby Blackpool.

On infrequent trips to London (something of a trek in those days) she showed a knowledge of the nation's capital which was remarkable.

My mum had a wicked sense of humour. No one loved a joke more than she did, and she was often caught in those heart-stopping moments when the room goes quiet, just as she was about to deliver the not-always-polite punch line. I have never laughed with anyone like I did with my mum. She only had to look at me in a certain way and we both set off and laughed until we cried and our stomachs ached.

Sometimes we laughed at something specific, like the Christmas morning when the man in the pew in front obviously needed to leave early and quietly but had difficulty getting his arm into the sleeve of his coat.

My mum turned to me and whispered 'he can't find his sleeve.' Don't ask me what was so funny about that, but we set off laughing and we laughed so much that we had to leave early too.

She was my dearest friend as well as my mum but she was strict as well. When she said something had to happen, she meant it. I was quite a biddable child and, anyway, I knew it was useless to argue with her. But my cousin Hilary always wanted her own way and usually got it from her worn down parents. Not with my mum. When Hilary started sounding off, mum would just give her one of her looks, and that would be an end of it.

I once came up against her, but never again. We were in a rather smart department store in St Annes. We'd moved to St Annes from the Lake District. In those days, department stores were the main places (if you were middle class) to shop for clothes. Most were on several floors and on each floor there was a manageress who sat at a desk ready to offer advice or to persuade doubtful shoppers that the outfit they were trying on was just the thing for them – or maybe not.

On the first floor of this particular store, the manageress was a very delightful lady called Mrs Pearce. We liked her a lot, but on that particular day a fit of devilment came over me and I pulled a horrid face at her. I'll never know why.

My mum marched me straight out of the shop and we got into the car which was parked nearby. 'Whatever did you think you were doing?' she demanded.

'I don't know,' I replied quite truthfully.

'Well,' said Mum, 'after lunch we'll go back and you will apologise to Mrs Pearce.'

'But it's my school party,' I protested.

'Yes,' said Mum, 'and you won't be going until you've said you're sorry to Mrs Pearce.'

The next two hours were some of the most miserable I can remember. All through lunch and during the statutory rest that kids had in those days, especially if they were going to a party, I was dreading what I had to do. Then I put on my blue net party frock (which had once belonged to Jill Brown, daughter of my Mum's friend Auntie Kath and the previous owner of the dolls' house) and my coat, and Mum and I returned to see Mrs Pearce.

I followed Mum up the stairs, feet as heavy as lead, to the first floor and there was Mrs Pearce, sitting at her desk and smiling her lovely smile.

I held Mum's hand tightly as she led me over.

'Diana has something to say to you, Mrs Pearce,' she said.

'I'm so sorry I pulled a face at you, I don't know why I did it. I didn't mean it,' I blurted out.

Mrs Pearce smiled even more. 'That's quite all right, Diana, and it's very brave of you to come back to apologise. Shall we see if there's something nice in my desk drawer for you?'

And out of the drawer, she pulled a bag of toffees and offered one to me. This was a treat indeed, since sweets were still rationed, and I danced off to the party with a light heart and a big mouthful of toffee. That taught me a valuable lesson I'll never forget.

As I grew up, my friends enjoyed coming to my house, as much for my mother's company as for mine.

One boyfriend who I finished with very amicably, left saying, 'I'm going to miss you, but I'll miss your mother too.'

I could have been a bit jealous but in fact, I was rather proud.

As well as being very attractive she was always smartly dressed and never went anywhere without her make-up. Her hair was immaculate. (Whatever happened to me, I wonder?). But this was only a veneer under which dwelt one of the kindest, funniest, most generous spirits you could ever meet.

*Rob in his areoplane in the Fleet Air
Arm. How he loved it!*

Chapter 5

A TRUE LIFE ROMANCE

With her looks and personality, my mother wasn't likely to be alone for long after my father left home. And sure enough, about a year later, a knight in shining armour came dramatically into her life – not on a white charger but in a sleek, white sports car, a Jaguar XK 120 – a beast never seen before in rural Westmorland, especially in this time of austerity.

Ian Appleyard was glamourous by anyone's standards – blond, blue-eyed and permanently tanned from frequent trips to Switzerland where he was hoping for a place in the British ski team for the winter Olympics of 1948. With her dark good looks, they made an attractive pair.

Not that it mattered to my mother, but he was also very rich. His father, Ernest, had started his working life mending bicycles in a modest way in Leeds, and like Lord Nuffield in Oxford, Ernest had steadily built up a motor business selling Jaguar cars which Ian had begun to drive, with great effect, in rallies all over Europe, eventually becoming Britain's top rally driver.

His success was also a good advertisement for the family business and today Appleyard of Leeds is still a thriving company.

It never occurred to me until much later, but Ian's success must have been a double delight to his parents, since his dearly loved and highly decorated eldest brother, Geoffrey, had been killed in action during the war. It must have also given Ian the driving force, in life as in motor sport, to be a success.

Aged five, I was unaware of all this but I really did like 'Uncle' Ian. He was good fun and he went out of his way to entertain me (well he would, wouldn't he, if he wanted a special place in my mother's affections).

He taught me to sit quietly by our bit of river watching for the bright flash of a kingfisher or to spot (much more difficult on account of its brown plumage) a dipper or water ousel on which he was an expert.

When we went to stay at his home, he let me help him to ring baby swallows so that he could check whether they returned next year. He bought me a beautiful book of British birds with illustrations by Charles Tunnicliffe, and I have it still.

He also took me for a drive in his car. It was not a

success. I had always suffered from car sickness and did so until I learnt to drive myself. I could just about manage at a slow pace in an ordinary saloon car but he took me in his great beast of a motor along the winding roads of the Lake District.

I'm sure he thought it would be a treat and for most children it would have been. But not for me. I threw up all over the beautiful red leather seats. He must have loved my mother. Maybe it was a test she set for him – he certainly passed with flying colours but I never went in that car again. And I still can't smell leather car seats without feeling queasy.

A trip to Ian's family home, the Manor House, Linton-in-Wharfdale, was a bit of an eye-opener. I think we must have gone on the train to avoid more travel sickness and I suppose I managed the short journey to their house in a more ordinary car.

My main memory of Linton Manor is that there were three bathrooms, one with a burgundy coloured suite. At home with my mother and grandparents, we had one bathroom (white) but many people in those days had none at all.

There were two maids, Laura and Mabel, who wore uniforms; Mabel was rather large and Laura was little and neat. They were very nice to me.

There was also a huge garden full of beautiful flowers. Ernest Appleyard said to me, 'You can pick any flower in the garden, Diana, except for the pink delphinium.'

All delphiniums were blue in those days and the pink one was his own invention. I was, as I have said, generally a good child so, of course, I didn't pick it.

It never occurred to me then – I was only five – that all these people were particularly kind to me because they wanted my mother to marry Ian. I could say that I resented him because he was taking the place of my father but it wouldn't be true – I never really connected the two. I was happy and I must have sensed that my mother was so I had no reason to put a spanner in the works.

All was going swimmingly. Ian was a regular visitor to our house in the Lakes and also after my grandparents and my mother moved back to their home town of St Annes-on-Sea where the social life was a bit more jolly.

One evening, Mummy and Ian were at a dance in the main hotel in St Annes and were sitting in a little balcony just above the dance floor with some of their friends. Then Mum was spotted by Rob, an old school friend of Uncle Joey, who had known her before the war.

He walked across the dance floor and asked her for a dance.

'Rob, how lovely to see you,' she said, came down

from the balcony and off they danced.

And that, really, was that. She left Ian, she left the millions and the high life and off she danced with Rob. It has to be said he was a very good dancer.

But it was absolutely the right decision. She and Rob had the happiest of marriages, which only ended with her far-too-early death at the age of 56. And he became not only my step-father but one of my closest friends.

His patience with a child seemed to be unlimited – when I was recovering from childhood diseases he helped me make endless cardboard models from the back of cornflake packets, every weekend in the holidays we would collect the cousins and go for a picnic somewhere he knew well and he would show us leaping salmon and where to pick bilberries and find grouse eggs.

He never minded when we got soaking wet in lakes and rivers and had to come home wrapped in his rather expensive travelling rugs. He endured journeys to and from boarding school, with me being sick with apprehension, and often came to get me from school on his own, so that mum could be at home with a hot and delicious meal on our arrival.

He sat beside me for hours in the passenger seat of his Hillman Minx while I practised my driving skills. Thanks to him I passed my driving test first time.

My mum died more than 40 years ago and I miss her still, but in a good way, a positive way. My great regret is that she never saw her grandchildren grow up – they were little girls when she died but it wasn't before they had both had wonderful holidays on their own with 'Gaga' who spoiled them as she had never dared to spoil me. And how she would have doted on her great grandchildren and they on her.

After she died, Rob and I were probably closer than ever. My two little girls used to love going to stay with him, even without my mum. He didn't do well on his own, though, and he married again but it wasn't the greatest success. When his second wife died he came down to the Cotswolds to live near us.

It was a very happy time during which he became a treasured member, not only of my family but also of my husband Malcolm's, whose daughters had never known either of their grandfathers and adopted Rob as their own.

Malcolm couldn't hear enough of Rob's stories of his time in the Fleet Air Arm during the war – something he had never talked about before; probably we'd never asked him.

Rob loved his time as a pilot when his job was to teach raw recruits how to fly on and off aircraft carriers bobbing about on the sea. Rob said, 'The deck looked like a postage stamp from the height where we were.'

And although he didn't get into any dogfights with German planes because that wasn't his job, we felt that his role was equally dangerous. He would have loved to have made a career in the Fleet Air Arm, but his father was a bully who made him come home to work in his accountancy firm. In those days you didn't argue with your parents.

Rob hated accountancy. He almost had a nervous breakdown when he was working for his exams and if it hadn't been for the fact that by then he had my mum's support and care he would have had the most miserable time. But because his home life was very happy he managed to stick it out as an accountant, even admitting that in the end he came to quite enjoy figures.

He had the gift of being particularly loveable and he and my mum had many friends but also enjoyed each other's company all their lives.

'Everybody loves Rob,' she used to say and they did. When he died we scattered his ashes on my mother's grave in Lancashire and on the Lakeland fells. I had no trouble thinking of an inscription to put on their joint gravestone made of a piece of Lakeland rock. "He was a man who everyone loved." And they did. Especially me.

Mum and Rob with the Daimler – a posh car bought very cheaply during a fuel crisis. I always found it rather an embarrassment

Chapter 6

THE FAMILY:
GRANNY AND GRANDPA

Apart from my mother – or as well as her, really – my grandparents were the most important people in my early childhood. I loved them unreservedly and they returned that love, and more.

It was just as well because we all lived together and living with grumpy grandparents must have been very difficult. My grandparents didn't do grumpy and I thought all adults were like them. It took me a long time to discover my mistake.

I remember being about nine and not being able to go to sleep because I was worried about Granny and Grandpa dying. I never considered my parents deaths because they were young, even in my childish world. But Granny and Grandpa – what would I do without them?

I got up and went to find my mother to tell her my worries and, in her usual way, she allayed my fears, although the same thoughts must have often occurred to her. In fact, they both lived to a ripe old age and it was my parents who were comparatively young when they died. By this time my mother had remarried and we no longer lived with Granny and Grandpa – we had a ground floor flat and they had the one upstairs …

Granny was a tiny little woman. 'I'm little and good,' she used to say, and she was.

But she would never divulge her age. 'I'm as old as my tongue and a little older than my teeth,' she would declare and that was all we ever got out of her – not for want of trying.

Even on her gravestone, her age doesn't appear, because nobody knew it. Well, maybe Grandpa did, but he wasn't saying.

Granny was a wonderful cook. Her cakes and scones, her homemade jam and lemon cheese were second to none and her roast dinners, particularly her gravy, were to die for. How she managed to provide for us as she did during the war and the subsequent austerity period, I shall never know. I have not inherited her baking skills – though my daughters have – but my gravy is pretty good and I have got her knack of providing meals for almost anyone who calls unexpectedly. I just have to.

I don't have her talents as a dressmaker, though; largely

because whenever I got in a mess with something I was sewing she would help me out, so I never really finished anything on my own. My mother was worse than me but we both wore beautiful clothes made by Granny. How she managed that in wartime is also a mystery.

She seldom used patterns – she looked at a dress or coat – that she liked and cut out the pattern for it in newspaper. My eldest daughter, Kate, never knew Granny, but she could do exactly the same with the result that, as a teenager, she had some remarkable clothes that I could not have afforded to buy her. And Emily has inherited her culinary skills so, for me Granny lives on.

Grandpa was fat and jolly. He looked like Winston Churchill and he was very proud when people remarked on this as they often did, particularly when he was on Home Guard duty during the war.

He was very musical and one of my earliest memories was sitting on his knee while he played nursery rhymes on the piano from books which I still treasure today. He had a fine base voice which made him much in demand with musical groups and he sang in the church choir until not long before he died. The choirmaster used to send a taxi for him when he got too infirm to walk far.

He loved his food. (And, apart from Granny, we were a family with very healthy appetites). Every Christmas day we used to watch in awe as he consumed turkey with all the trimmings, Christmas pudding, mince pies and even managed Lancashire cheese at the end – 'just a nip, thank you, dear' – washed down with 'good' red wine. Then he would sleep till it was time for supper and start again …

Grandpa was a pushover as far as persuading him to let me get up to mischief was concerned. Of the many times we got into trouble together, one incident particularly springs to mind. He had been left in charge of me while Mum and Granny went out – they must have forgotten the hazards of doing this, or maybe there was no one else around.

'Now, little Chummykins,' he said (he used my nickname until he died, by which time I was married, with children of my own). 'What would you like to do today?'

I was about four at the time but I already had a plan. 'You know that steep bank at the side of the house, Grandpa? Well I would really love to climb to the top of it and slide down, if you could catch me at the bottom.'

Of course he agreed and we spent a jolly afternoon as I climbed to the top of the bank, slid down and he caught me. Up and down I went as the bank, which was in the shade and always damp, got muddier and muddier. We didn't hear Mum and Granny come home until we heard their gasps of horror.

If I had been a modern child, sensibly dressed in jeans or dungarees, it wouldn't have been so bad, but I had on a white muslin frock with blue spots and knickers to match.

The frock survived but it was a very long time before Grandpa and I were left on our own again.

Both Granny and Grandpa were wonderful storytellers. Granny used to tell me tales about a mechanical doll called Jane who was always up to mischief. Probably that was where I got some of my ideas for my exploits with Grandpa.

She would also tell me tales of when my mother and my Uncle Joey were young. I loved these although I could never quite imagine them as children. When she ran out of ideas she would read to me from the stories by Alison Uttley about Little Grey Rabbit who lived in a dear little house on the edge of a wood with her rather selfish friends, Squirrel and Hare.

Little Grey Rabbit always reminded me of Granny because she was so kind – and she was always cooking or sewing.

But best of all was when she read me the tales of Beatrix Potter because we lived among those very lakes and mountains which she had painted in her illustrations, and it wasn't hard to picture Mrs Tiggy Winkle delivering washing around Helvellyn or Squirrel Nutkin 'sailing' on Lake Windermere.

When their own children were young Granny and Grandpa used to rent a cottage for the summer holidays in the village of Sawrey, where Beatrix Potter lived. Granny used to tell me how she often saw Beatrix Potter loading her Herdwick sheep onto the ferry to go to the market in Kendal. 'She was usually wearing an old black hat with a sack over her shoulders and she was calling those sheep names which didn't appear in any of her books …'

Grandpa's stories were about a group of pixies who lived in Abbot Hall, a real house not far from ours and whose main task – apart from getting up to a lot of mischief – was to go out with tins of white paint in the middle of the night and repaint the white lines on the road. Hey ho! Hey ho!

But what I loved best as I grew up was to talk to him about history which was my favourite subject – because he had lived it.

'Tell me about when the Great War broke out,' I would ask him and he would start by telling me all the political stuff. Then he would relate exactly what he had been doing and where he was on that particular day so that to me it was real and not just a few dry facts in a book.

It was much later in life, when talking to other people about their grandparents that I realised just how lucky I was.

*One of Rob's picnics in the Fells. Granny,
Mum, me and Winnie the Pooh*

*Granny and Mum are wearing suits – on
a country walk! I'm in a frock and Pooh
Bear is wearing the famous white muslin
dress with the blue spots*

Grandpa as a young man

*In the garden with Hilary and
assorted toys*

Chapter 7

THE REST OF THE FAMILY

Ours was a very small family because my mother and her brother had both married another pair of siblings. This meant that my cousins, Martin and Hilary, and I had nearly identical DNA (although Crick and Watson had yet to crack the double helix and DNA wasn't known about at that time). We also shared the same two sets of grandparents, which didn't seem at all strange to us because we thought all cousins had the same.

Because I was an only child and came in age between the two of them we saw a lot of each other. Hilary was the constant companion of my childhood – we played together, rode horses together, played tennis together, went constantly to the cinema together and spent holidays with one another. We never went to the same school, though (I've often wondered why).

We weren't at all alike – Hilary was dark haired while I was fair, and tall and slim while I was short and plump and our temperaments couldn't have been more different. She was a tricky customer, our Hilary; she liked to have things her own way and she usually got them, though not with my mother as I've already mentioned.

I was probably the worst possible companion for her because I just didn't care – it was usually much easier to go along with what she wanted to do, though I did object when she grabbed my precious Larry Lamb from me and put him in her dolls' pram. But it was probably a salutary lesson for me to learn that the world wasn't just filled with people like my Mum and Dad and Granny and Grandpa. And I never giggled with anyone, except my Mum, as I did with Hilary. We remained firm friends until the end of her life. I miss her still. A lot.

Martin was very different. We both had similar easy going temperaments and our friendship really grew when Hilary went off to college and we went to ballroom dancing classes together and spent a good part of our holidays huddled with a group of friends in Don's Record Shop listening to the latest in the Top Twenty.

Hilary would not have approved – she was studying music at the Royal College in Manchester and had become an evangelical Christian, so she wouldn't have liked the parties we went to either. Although he was younger than me, he didn't look it and he rescued me from several unwanted admirers who didn't know he was my cousin.

Martin had caught polio when he was eight – the dreaded infantile paralysis which could cause death or serious disability. There was a national epidemic after the war, before the vaccine was available. For several days he was on the danger list in the local isolation hospital as the paralysis crept up his arm. Then miraculously it stopped and everyone smiled again.

He was left far from unscathed and has suffered a lot of pain. But I have never known him to complain or to let his disability stop him from doing what he intended to do in life. I admire him enormously and I also regard him as one of my very best friends. We've had so much fun together and he still spends Christmas with us, together with his son, Tom, and his grandchildren.

There's no doubt that the head of the family was Uncle Joey, their father. He was my mother's brother and Granny and Grandpa's only son. Granny worshipped him and consulted him on almost everything.

'I'm not God, Mother,' he used to say but I'm not sure that she believed him.

When my dad left home, Uncle Joey rather took over my mother's and my lives and I'm sure it was he who decreed that I should go to boarding school, which

I hated. But as he was also responsible for me getting to university, which I really loved, I never bore him any malice.

In fact I loved him a lot and he really was a father figure until my mother married again.

Uncle Joey was married to Auntie Stella who was small and rather excitable and not at all like my dad, her brother. But the thing they had in common was the ability to laugh at themselves and Auntie Stella used to have us in stitches with stories of scrapes she'd got into – usually in connection with her rather erratic driving.

She was a very talented musician and was much in demand as an accompanist at local music festivals – which I learnt later is a great skill. She also sang in choirs and was an active member of the local operatic society. When she died, my uncle gave a bursary in her name to the Royal Northern College of Music in Manchester and the Stella Bradshaw Trophy is presented to this day.

Our other granny, Nana, was also small and rather excitable and I didn't see much of her when I was growing up because she refused to speak to my mother who had had the temerity to leave her beloved son. Nana doted on my dad as much as Granny did on Uncle Joey.

This state of affairs lasted until I was about 16 when Nan was about to move house and Auntie Stella had a nervous breakdown so my mother went to help her instead. Whereupon they fell into each other's arms and cried and were firm friends ever after. Nan even grew to love my stepfather, Rob, who was a particularly lovable man and who used to do all sorts of jobs for her when her beloved son wasn't around. It taught me a valuable lesson – that forgiveness is always possible if you want it enough.

Nan spoiled us all rotten. She cooked us delicious meals, in spite of being badly crippled with arthritis, and gave us £5 when Hilary, Martin and I went back to school or college. 'Little tips, darlings,' she would say pressing the big white notes into our eager hands. In those days it was a massive "tip".

All through our childhood and well beyond, mystery surrounded our other grandfather who rejoiced in the name of Hodgeson Hewitt Lancaster. He had left Nan when her children were young and she never spoke of him. I always thought she was a widow and she never said anything to make me believe otherwise.

It was my mother who told me later what had actually happened but she had no idea what had become of him. Daddy was in touch with him, she thought, but I was so busy getting on with my life that I never asked him – one of the many things I never got round to discussing with him before he died of a massive heart attack aged only 62, while staying with us in the Cotswolds.

It was only when Hilary, Martin and I were approaching middle age ourselves that we became more curious about Hodgeson Hewitt Lancaster. After all, with a name like that he shouldn't be too hard to find. Egged on by Malcolm, my husband, who seemed to be far more interested in him than we were, we began a rather half-hearted search.

I was sure my mum had told me that he had once worked for the Blackpool Tram Company as one of the bosses, but a phone call from Malcolm to their archive department drew a blank.

The trail went cold for several years, largely due to the apathy of those who were supposed to be searching. It was only when websites dedicated to tracing one's ancestors began to appear that Hilary started to uncover some facts about our elusive grandfather. But she never told Martin or me. In her defence, I think she was getting too deep into the depressive illness which eventually caused her death and it was only when Martin was sorting through her papers after she had died that he found the notes she had made on HHL.

It appears that he had left Nana, who I suspect he had married for her money, for an Irishwoman, Helen Dora Megaffin. He married Helen in Leeds in 1931. He died in London in 1944, aged 58, and probate was granted in Llandudno in 1945. Why did they move to London, and why was probate granted in Llandudno? What happened to them during those years? We shall never know. Helen lived until 1975, dying only three years before my father.

Further enquiries to the Blackpool Tram Company and a rather more forthcoming archivist revealed that my grandfather had indeed once worked there but it was his father, John Lancaster, who was the company boss.

My grandfather actually held a much more junior position until his flight from the north west with Helen. Was he perhaps escaping from the influence of a dominating father?

The mystery remained, but Martin and I were rather delighted to finally know that in our immediate family of lovely but extremely conventional people (my father excepted), we actually had a proper black sheep.

My extended family was quite colourful, however. The Johnsons, who are my cousins, played a big part in our lives and still do. They were frequent visitors throughout my childhood but it was only as an adult that I really began to appreciate them properly.

Granny was one of seven children – Cissie, whose real name was Clara and after whom my mother was named Claire, brought up her younger siblings after their mother's untimely death. Jack emigrated to Australia; Freddie was killed with so many others in the battle of the Somme; Frank was rather too fond of the cards and the horses; and Walter founded a school for the blind in Bradford. Next came Granny and finally Auntie Edith who later emigrated to Canada where her son became an eminent musician.

Granny loved them all, though she often despaired of Frank and was very supportive of his wife, Auntie Annie and their five children. But her real favourite was Uncle Walter and, among her many nieces and nephews she particularly loved Uncle Walter's son, Vin.

Vin was the youngest of five boys – he was the same age as Uncle Joey and only a little older than my mother. He spent a lot of time with our family, particularly during the summer holidays in the Lake District, and the mutual affection that Granny and Vin had for one another lasted all their lives. I remember that Granny's Christmas Day was never quite complete until Vin had rung.

He later told me that in the early days it meant trudging more than a mile to the nearest phone box, often in awful weather, until the phone was installed in the remote Yorkshire cottage where he lived with his wife Mary and their three children, Philip, Richard and Claire, named after my mother.

Mary was something else. She was Irish, dark haired

and blue eyed and not entirely approved of at first by Granny because she was "in trade", the rag trade, no less. At that time, even after the war when middle class women increasingly went out to work, they usually became teachers or secretaries and often gave up any thought of a career when they had children. In the Johnson's case, it was Vin who was the teacher, taking up his profession after he was demobbed from the army at the end of the war.

'I had to work as well, darling, or we wouldn't have had enough to live on,' Mary told me many years later. But she was extremely good at what she did, holding down a job in the fashion department of a prestigious department store in Bradford and later being head hunted by the exclusive fashion house of Cresta and made manager of their shop in Bristol's fashionable Park Street. Mary arrived in Bristol just as I was finishing my first year as a student there and so began a particularly close friendship between the Johnsons, my friends, and my own young family. It has so enriched our lives, and what laughs we've had.

It was sheer chance that Mary's arrival in Bristol to start her new job and to house hunt coincided with my friend Sally and I having to leave our digs, as they were called in those days, because our landlady's husband had gone bankrupt. As we were about to take our first part final exams, my mother, who had come down to sort us out, deemed it most unsuitable for us to doss down on a friend's floor at that particular time. Mary, meanwhile, had booked herself in at the local YWCA (Young Women's Christian Association) so Mum decided we should go there too and we all went for an interview with the Warden, Mrs Muller, who would not have been out of place overseeing a German prisoner of war camp.

No men beyond the first stair and the doors locked at 11pm. Having both escaped from boarding school the previous year, this was certainly not what Ada and I had in mind.

But the presence of Mary with her ability to see the funny side of everything made our lives bearable for the time we were there and when we finally escaped Frau Muller's clutches, I went to stay in the flat which Mary had found for the family to move down to.

For the remaining two years that I was a student in Bristol, the Johnson's flat, which was about 20 minutes' walk from where I lived, became a haven for me. When I just needed a bit of family cossetting and a change of company, I would walk over there, spend a hilarious evening with them and go back to student life invigorated.

I didn't manage to go there on my own very often, though. When I was unwise enough to mention where I was going to my inner circle of friends, they wanted to come with me and we used to talk to Vin and Mary until late into the night when Vin would pack us into the back of his little van and take us back to our various homes.

By this time their son Philip had joined us. Philip had mischief oozing out of every pore – you simply never knew what he would be up to next but he was a lot of fun – and I, when relieved of the rigours of exams, was more than happy to join in. Mary also entered into the spirit of the general hilarity – even when we shut her in the larder.

She was full of sayings, oft quoted by the rest of the family, the most frequent being, 'That's life kid'. It was her standard reply when someone was grumbling about their lot, and then she would sum up the scale of the disaster with: 'Nobody's dead'.

And really there was no answer to that.

It would be easy to talk about my family without mentioning Auntie Elsie. She was such a self-effacing little soul that we hardly knew she was there. Auntie Elsie was Grandpa's only sister and their parents had not allowed her to marry or to train for a career since they considered that her purpose in life was to look after them in their old age.

'We shall leave you well provided for, Elsie dear,' they said, but of course they didn't.

A world war followed by a slump put paid to that, and

although she was a talented musician and artist, she was left with no money and no qualifications so that her only option was to become a companion to crabby old ladies, who certainly didn't appreciate her as she deserved.

She was not, of course, alone in that, but was one of many, many women who had been cast on the scrap heap of life by selfish, thoughtless parents. I think of her whenever I hear a woman complaining about their lot in life today.

She spent most of her meagre holidays with us and she was very interesting to talk to once she came out of her shell. She always reminded me of a little woodland creature, ready to run away to safety when danger threatened.

When she retired, Uncle Joey bought her a flat and the smile never left her face when she had her own home at last. But I was sad when I visited her to see in the corner of her sitting room the trunk into which she had packed all her worldly belongings as she moved from one job to another. She covered it with a rug but it was always there, just in case.

My Granny gave Auntie Elsie her own rocking chair to help to furnish the flat. I have it now and I can still see that tiny, grey unobtrusive figure dozing to its rhythm – safely home at last.

Devoted siblings – Mum and Uncle Joey

The Johnson Family in 1953:
Vin, Philip, Claire, Richard (Ricky) and Mary

Chapter 8

THE FAMILY: LITTLE MARY

The cast list of my family would not be complete without Little Mary. Mary hated being called 'little', though she was, if anything, smaller than both the grannies, but we called her that, out of earshot, to distinguish her from Cousin Mary Johnson (who was rather tall).

Little Mary was not a relation but she was a vital member of our family. In those days she was known as our 'help', today we'd call her our cleaning lady – she certainly did a lot more than simply helping.

Mary came to see my granny for an interview when I was five and they agreed on a month's trial either way to make sure they both got on with one another. By noon on her first morning I went to ask Granny if I could have my lunch (we called it dinner up there) with Mary.

As we all sat down together Granny said, 'I think we can forget about the month's trial, don't you, Mary?'

Mary agreed. She finally retired about 40 years later,

having worked for every member of the family but particularly for Granny and later for Mum.

Mary came from Workington in Cumberland. She left school at 13 to go into service and her first job every morning at 6am for the family she worked for was to black the grates and get the fires going. She always said that she was lucky – her 'family' treated her well, unlike the employers of some of her friends. Since then, she and her husband had worked for a friend of Granny's who ran a small hotel but that was about to close. How lucky was that for us?

When Mary cleaned she was like a Whirling Dervish and the older she got the faster she seemed to whirl. But she was certainly thorough. Who would count scrubbing the front step and washing the garden gate among their normal chores today?

She had a vocabulary all her own, some of which has survived thanks to our family's perhaps rather off the wall sense of humour. One of these was when the world around her seemed to be going mad.

'It's kiosk,' she would announce and it's a word that survives among us to this day.

My mother often forgot and used it in public to the bemusement of many, especially the young man behind the Post Office one very busy day just before Christmas.

If it was raining hard, to Mary it was 'torriental' – and

years later, to us, it still is. But in spite of leaving school at 13 she was an excellent speller – unlike my mother and me – and we never had to reach for the dictionary when she was around.

Long after my Granny died, Mary remained a big part of my family (still working). The thing which makes me very happy is that she played a part in my children's lives too, and they still remember the bags of jelly babies she would bring for them when she knew they were staying with my mum and dad.

Chapter 9

ROB'S FAMILY

My stepdad Rob was an only child with a widowed mother and only a very few relations but they are all etched very clearly in my memory.

Nellie Smith, or Step-Granny as I called her, was quite unlike either of the other grannies, being tall and rather shy. She had qualified as a teacher and taught until she had married. This would be thought very strange today when women continue in their careers through marriage and motherhood, but back then it was even stranger that she'd had a career at all. It was expected of middle-class women that they would stay at home to look after their families.

Many women of her class and generation were qualified for nothing. If they married they had to learn to be wives and mothers as they went along. And if, like my poor Auntie Elsie, they were not even allowed to try to qualify for a career, unless they came from a super-rich family they were often left with precious little to live on after their parents died.

With Step-Granny, it was different. Her mother had died when she was very young and she was brought up by five maiden aunts who had a very different view of life and insisted that she should be independent. So young Nellie Smith left Lancashire in 1904 to travel to Bristol Day Training College in the Redland area of the city. Sixty years later, I came to know the city very well myself when it was my turn to pursue education. I still have one of her college books and I treasure it. My Step-Granny, shy as she was, was in the forefront of what later became a huge movement for women's rights, which still continues to this day.

She was very sporty and I have a picture of her in the college hockey team. In later life she learned to play golf and had a selection of trophies in her house. But sadly she married a man who was a bit of a bully and was later unfaithful to her, though it was never mentioned of course. Her husband, known to my mum and me as the late lamented Bramwell, died the same year as mum married Rob so I didn't know him at all. But my mum went to work on Step-Granny, persuaded her to buy fashionable clothes and generally to spend some money on herself.

'What a change in Nellie since Bram died,' one of her

Bridge Club friends said to my mother one day. 'But it's all due to you dear.' And it was.

Step-Granny never threw anything away and it used to drive my mother to distraction. But for me it was wonderful. I was very involved with drama at school and her old clothes were the staple of the school theatre wardrobe.

'I can't get hold of a such and such,' our drama teacher would say, 'do you think your granny would have one?'

And she always did. 'I knew that they'd come in handy one day,' she would say, much to my mother's despair.

Step-Granny, like the other grannies, was a wonderful cook. I shall never forget the goose she roasted every New Year, and her lemon meringue pie was to die for. She remained very fit for most of her life and kept her brain active by playing bridge which she did until she was in her nineties and grew too deaf to trump Mrs Mallinson's ace any more.

She lived on her own, visited every day by Rob, and walked to the shops to get her own groceries with a spring in her step which belied her enormous age. She was also an avid reader and, like me, her favourite writer was Jane Austen. My last conversation with her was when she was 99 and very deaf but we managed fine. She died three months short of her 100th birthday and her late teenage step-grandchildren, of whom she was very fond, were at her funeral. Rob, by this time, was 72.

Rob and Step-Granny didn't have many relations by the time we knew them but the four I did know are forever etched on my memory. Three of them were Uncle William and Auntie Martha, the late lamented Bramwell's bachelor brother and widowed sister, and Auntie Martha's younger son Granville. It was far too much to say their names every time so they were always known as Fence, the village outside Burnley where they lived.

Because they had no telephone they would turn up without letting us know and always at an inappropriate moment, such as Wimbledon finals day when mum and I were glued to our tiny black and white television. We would suddenly be aware that we were being watched and looked up to see them smiling and waving at the window …

I really loved Granville who reminded me of a great woolly teddy bear. We found that we had the same birthday and sent cards to one another all his life. He was a schoolteacher too and I always wished I'd been in his class. Uncle William looked like a character from a Dickens novel and was always a rather shadowy figure while Auntie Martha was little and plump and very, very deaf.

She had a hearing aid which hung round her neck and

was attached to numerous batteries, but it didn't seem very effective, even when she gave them a good shake. Auntie Martha's eldest son, Raymond, was the clever one of the family. He was a Maths Wrangler from Cambridge and became professor of Maths at Manchester University, following in the footsteps of the great Alan Turing, the cracker of the enigma code.

Sometimes Fence were accompanied by Cousin Martha Anne Radford from Bacup, a town about as Lancashire as you could get. I've no idea whose cousin she was but she was called Cousin Martha to distinguish her from Auntie Martha. She had a very loud voice and used to grab me by each cheek and say what a bonny girl I was.

On one memorable occasion, Step-Granny made the mistake of inviting both Marthas to stay with her - for a week. On the day they left, my mother found Step-Granny lying on her sofa with a damp cloth on her forehead.

On being asked what was wrong, she replied, 'Auntie Martha couldn't hear and Cousin Martha shouted louder than ever. I shall never have them to stay together again.'

Chapter 10

THE FAMILY FANCY DRESS

I must have been about eight and Hilary ten when we decided to organise a family fancy dress party. I don't know where we got the idea from – probably one of our books, as we were both avid readers by then.

We recruited Mum, Rob, Granny and Grandpa – Martin was deemed too young to take part – and we held it in the sitting room of the flat which we then rented, below the one where Granny and Grandpa lived. Granny organised a splendid tea with lots of sandwiches and homemade cakes and we sorted out costumes for everybody.

We dressed Grandpa up as a snowman in a large white sheet and a red scarf and Granny was a flower seller complete with a basket of flowers which she had collected for decorating her hats. I went as a sailor girl in my dress which Granny had made from a blackout curtain used during the war and Hilary wore her jodhpurs. I can't remember what Mum and Rob dressed up as at that party.

It was a great success (Hilary and I thought so anyway) and it became an annual event for the next few years, I suspect stretching the imaginations of the grown-ups rather more than they may have wanted, although they were always very good natured about taking part.

In the end we decided we would have one last family fancy dress – I think we were all running out of ideas. I burst into the sitting room wearing my finery – I think that year it was a Robin Hood outfit that dear Granny had made for me for the end of term party at school – to find that Mum and Rob hadn't dressed up at all. I do remember feeling a bit disappointed – they might have made an effort this last time.

But closer inspection revealed that they had made a great effort as each had dressed up as the other …

Mum looked rather splendid in Rob's tweed suit and trilby hat and Rob had taken the trouble to wear a jumper and skirt that Mum often wore, so we couldn't mistake who he was. He looked pretty good from the knees upwards but his hairy legs and bedroom-slippered feet were a bit of a giveaway when we looked at him more closely. Even so it was a good effort in order to entertain two little girls and one of the first of many times that I realised what really good sports my Mum and Rob were.

Mum, Rob and me dressed to kill for a wedding.
My outfit was in 'African violet', the 'in' colour of
the time

Second from left. The fattest fairy in the
school play at Androssen. Note the high
wall around the joyless playground

Chapter 11

LITTLE SCHOOL

I have no idea who chose the schools I went to – four in all – but they were certainly a mixed bag. One was horrible, one was the happiest place I've ever set foot in, one was very odd and one was fine, except that it was a boarding school and I hated being away from home. But, like most other things in life, I got used to it.

I started at Ardrossen Preparatory School when I was five. It was without doubt the most joyless place I have every been to, but I suppose I thought all schools were like that and I expect many still were in those days. One of my abiding memories of Ardrossen was that it was tall and narrow. Tall, narrow classrooms, tall, narrow playground and a curriculum that was just narrow.

It was run by two spinsters, Miss Nicholson and her younger sister, Miss Marjorie as we called her, as though we were still in the Victorian age. I don't know what had happened to Miss Nicholson earlier in her life but it had made her a bitter and vindictive woman; I think Miss Marjorie would have been quite good fun if she'd been allowed – but she wasn't. Nicholson is an unfortunate name for a head teacher and inevitably she was nicknamed Knickers. It rather suited her.

I don't know if either if them had any teaching qualifications – it probably wasn't necessary in those days when OFSTED inspections were in the distant future and I'm not sure if privately run schools were subject to the dreaded HM Inspector. I can't imagine he would have warmed to Ardrossen.

I can't actually remember any lessons except arithmetic and painting (you couldn't call it art). Arithmetic was frightening. Miss Nicholson rattled away and put example sums on the blackboard. We then had to try them ourselves and Get Them Right.

I seldom did and she never really explained where I had gone wrong – or perhaps I was in so much of a panic by this time that I couldn't take it in. She would threaten us with detention until we had got them right – I think my mother put a stop to that or goodness knows how long she would have been waiting for me at the end of each day.

At the weekend we had arithmetic homework and my uncle Joey used to help me with it. Somehow, when he explained how it all worked I could understand immediately but when I got back to school with Miss Knickers making sarcastic remarks, I forgot it all again. During most of my school life I was convinced that I was innumerate but I think it was simply the way I was first taught – I seem to have managed perfectly well since.

Painting came as a real relief but we would never have become artists as a result. We each had a little painting book with pictures already in it, a box of paints and a jar of water. Miss Marjorie came round to each of us and dabbed the colour from the paint box on to a certain bit of the picture which we then had to fill in. When we had done this we had to wait till she came round again and repeated the process – it hardly expanded our artistic horizons.

We must have done some form of English but I was so unnerved by the maths that I can't remember it and we certainly did drama of a sort because I have a photograph of a group of us dressed up as fairies (I was by far the fattest).

We had no outdoor games, just a few minutes in the crowded, narrow, tarmacked playground, with a drink of milk, before being summoned back indoors for more lessons. There were no school dinners so we all went home for lunch, thank goodness. At least it made a break in the tedious school day.

Every morning and afternoon Miss Marjorie (always the dogsbody) would come into both classrooms carrying a large spray full of some kind of disinfectant and spray the contents into the air so that they fell on us like a shower. I suppose it was to combat germs in those crowded classrooms but I can't remember it being very successful – I contracted measles, mumps and whooping cough while I was there – inoculations were a thing of the future but being ill was a bonus because it meant that I didn't have to go to school.

Miss Nicholson was a stickler for uniform – it had to be exactly right – and that was her undoing. One summer day one of the girls arrived wearing a non-regulation dress. It had blue and white stripes like the others but it wasn't exactly the same. I imagine she had spilled something on her school dress the night before and her mother hadn't had it ready in time.

Knickers made this poor girl stand on a chair in front of the whole school and told us that if anyone else ever, ever, came to school in the 'wrong' uniform they would be taken away in a black van and would never see their parents again.

People to whom I have told this story have looked totally disbelieving but it really was true. The incident happened in the morning and we all went home to lunch and told our parents about it.

My mother was never one to stand idly by. She telephoned my uncle, who was a solicitor and whose office was a few doors away from the school, and a stern letter was hand delivered to the Miss Nicholsons that afternoon. I have no idea what it said but the result of the incident was that a group of us left Ardrossen and never went back. They included the Airey family who lived just up the road from us and with whom I played most days and the Beamonts, also friends, whose father was a famous pilot who had fought in the Battle of Britain and was the first man to fly to the US and back in a day. I bet old Knickers was furious to lose them.

I'm not sure what the repercussions were for the school but for those of us who left it was a defining moment when we learnt that gown ups didn't always stick together and that what children said sometimes really could change things. For us, life was about to change and very much for the better.

A group of from Ardrossen – and I can't remember exactly who they were, except for Carol, Heather and Peter Airey – started at the School in the Sun in the autumn of 1950. With its large, airy classrooms which faced the sea and its atmosphere of joy and fun, it couldn't have been a greater contrast from what we had become used to.

Our uniforms at Ardrossen had been grey and dark blue – at the School in the Sun they were grey and bright orange and on the school badge was embroidered the smiling face of the sun. That really summed up the difference.

The school was run by Mr and Mrs Milnes who were artists and most of what we did was connected to painting and craft. Mrs Milnes was also very musical and we did a lot of singing – not that she taught me to sing in tune, nobody ever managed that.

To the casual onlooker it would seem that we weren't learning much but I still remember the things I learnt there. We had history painting, colouring in classic historical pictures such as The Boyhood of Raleigh, and geography painting where we recreated the colourful costumes of people from all over the world (which was largely the British Empire in those days).

Nobody told us what colours to use – what we were encouraged to use was our imagination. That was a welcome change. On warm summer days we took stools, drawing books and pastels and drew the quaint little fishermens' cottages in the streets of Lytham, and in winter Mr Milnes would show us a famous painting, give us a pile of sticky paper shapes and some stiff paper and encourage us to recreate the painting with them.

I'm not sure how recognisable they were when we'd finished but it gave us a knowledge of the Great Masters at a very early age.

We weren't aware that we were being taught maths but on the bright yellow walls of the classroom 'times tables' were written in blue chalk. We could see them all day except when Mr Milnes covered them up and gave us a test in which we all knew the answers because we weren't made to feel nervous about getting them wrong.

He would read Aesop's fables and Kipling's Just So Stories to us and then get us to write the story in our own words – I still remember them too. For spelling practise he would teach us to correct the words we had got wrong in our stories. One boy couldn't get to grips with the spelling of 'water' (it must have been in his re-telling of the Story of the Armadillo) and insisted on writing 'worter'.

'No, Geoffrey, no,' said Mr Milnes, getting as near as I ever witnessed to mild impatience. 'It doesn't have worts.'

As well as teaching us to sing patriotic songs like The Roast Beef of Old England and all the verses of what was then God save the King, Mrs Milnes soon progressed to Sur le Pont d'Avignon, Frere Jacques, the Brahams Lullaby and Stille Nacht. It was a wonderful way of introducing children to other languages.

At break time we collected a bottle of milk and a delicious bun from Miss Lemesurier, the housekeeper, and Mr and Mrs Milnes saw us all across the road to get rid of our pent up energy on Lytham Green. For those who have never been there, Lytham has the longest green in the country – it stretches for almost a mile along the sea front and there is a tall, white windmill half way along.

This was our playground – what a contrast from the narrow little yard at Ardrossen. A great excitement was when the huge, white banana boats would sail past on their way to Preston docks and when dirty old dredgers would chug up and down the estuary, making sure that all the shipping could get up and down. The lifeboat played an important part in the life of a seaside community and I remember the day when we all trouped down to one of the jetties to watch the launching of the new lifeboat. I didn't know then but the Royal National Lifeboat Institution was founded after an appalling tragedy in the Ribble estuary where two lifeboats were lost. On the seafront at St Annes (Lytham and St Annes were separate towns but were united as one borough) there was a statue of a lifeboat man on a tall plinth, looking out to sea, to commemorate the tragic event. I loved that lifeboatman and regarded him as my friend.

After break we would go back for more 'lessons' and then lunch which Miss Lemesureier cooked and which was always delicious. I remember that Mr Milnes listened to the news on a large wireless so we listened too. I suppose this was our current affairs lesson. The shipping forecast came first and we listened to that as well. I always feel nostalgic when I hear it today. For seaside communities the weather and shipping forecasts were of great importance, as was the weather itself. When I was in bed on a foggy night I could hear the fog horns hooting in the estuary and I always hoped that the boats would be safe and not run aground on the treacherous mud flats.

When afternoon lessons were over we rushed over to the green again to let off steam before going home. I realise now what sensible people the Milnes were. They had no children of their own but they seemed instinctively to know what was best for a child. I think I probably learned more in the year I spent at the School in the Sun than at any other time in my life – and quite without realising it – even though it might not have passed the OFSTED inspection either.

The final joy of the day was going home on the bus without having to wait to be collected by our parents (I expect they were quite joyful about it too). Every day

I went to school and came home on the bus with my own special little book of bus tickets and then walked the last short stretch to our house. How grown up and independent I felt.

I never did find out what happened to Ardrossen because I really didn't care, but I heard that the Milnes' eventually retired. Mrs Milnes died and later Mr Milnes married Miss Lemesurier. So the story of a happy school had a happy ending, I'm glad to say.

At the end of the year I left to go to boarding school. It was a good job I had no idea what it would be like.

Chapter 12

A NASTY SHOCK

In the excitement of buying a new uniform, the enormity of what was about to happen to me rather passed me by. (This time the uniform was maroon and grey and included a most unflattering gymslip and an equally ugly grey gabardine mackintosh).

There were all sorts of other articles of clothing I'd never seen before, such as grey gym knickers under which ordinary white knickers were worn – they were known as 'linings'. And the shoes! There were outdoor shoes, indoor shoes, hockey boots, gym shoes, wellington boots and bedroom slippers. I'd never possessed so much footwear in the whole of my short life.

Every item had to be named and, apart from the shoes which were written on with a black ink pen, they all required a nametape. This would have been a tremendous chore for my mother who hated sewing, but Granny came to the rescue and sewed on hundreds of nametapes with neat stitches.

As the day of departure drew nearer, these were all packed neatly into a small green trunk. Why did it never occur to me that taking all this stuff meant that I would be away from home for weeks at a time?

Of course, my mother explained all this to me but I was far too excited to listen. And so it was that in mid-September 1951 the green trunk was loaded into the family Hillman and off we set for North Wales, through the Mersey Tunnel and out into the mountainous Welsh countryside, heading for the seaside resort of Llandudno.

It was a beautiful day and the sun sparkled on the sea. We walked along the Promenade and watched a Punch and Judy show. By this time I was clutching a brown rabbit wearing blue trousers and a white shirt which Mummy had bought for me in the town that day.

I still have him although I think he's in a rather inaccessible part of my loft, together with Pooh Bear, who by this time had a maroon and grey uniform, knitted by kind Granny. She (my bear was a girl and not a boy like Christopher Robin's Pooh) was to be my constant companion for the rest of my young life and how I needed her during those first weeks at school. She is in no one's loft but sits in splendour, looking rather well worn, on top of a cupboard in my daughter Kate's London house. She is now over seventy years old.

The time came to drive to the school and I still had no idea what was about to befall me. Gloddaeth Hall was a Tudor manor house not far out of the town but surrounded by spectacular countryside. There was part of a moat still surrounding it and beautifully manicured gardens with the playing fields beyond.

It had belonged to the Mostyn family and their coat of arms appeared on the numerous stained glass windows in the house. I think there were about 150 girls aged from eight to sixteen, and mostly we slept in small dormitories on the first floor. I, however, had been put in the old billiard room where there were twelve iron beds in two rows, each covered with a very inadequate mattress and a grey army blanket, with the inevitable stained glass window at one end.

It didn't look cosy but luckily we had brought our own bedding and eiderdowns (remember them?) which cheered the room a bit. The bed next to mine had been allocated to the single soul I knew there at the time. She was christened Alison but was mysteriously known as Diggy by her parents who were friends of my mother's. Diggy was the reason I'd been sent to the school in the first place – how incredible that seems in this day of choosing schools for their academic reputation. Diggy had red hair and freckles and a temper to match. We were good friends but I did come to wish she didn't snore.

The time came for our parents to say goodbye. 'We'll see you in three weeks time and then we'll have a lovely weekend together,' said my mum in rather a tearful voice and Rob hugged me for longer than usual.

Still it didn't really sink in that they were going home without me. Diggy got the message, though, and she howled loudly until her parents were out of sight. She did this all the time we were at school.

It was time for supper and the younger girls were all herded into the Junior Dining Room. This was probably one of the most cheerful rooms in the building because the walls were decorated with a frieze of the Pied Piper of Hamelin, dressed from top to toe in yellow and red and followed by a band of children with the little lame boy at the end.

It was the only cheerful thing about that dining room – the food was almost inedible. That first night we had slices of cold lamb which consisted mainly of fat and a rather soggy salad. There were jugs of salad cream on the table and the one I used had a large drowned bluebottle in it. It wasn't a good start and it didn't improve. We just got used to it and I am still the least fussy eater I know. We had all taken our ration books with us but I can't believe that they were ever used for the food we ate.

And so to bed, supervised by the school matron,

Sister Hopper, who had a sharp tongue in her head and wasn't afraid to use it. Unfortunately, her room was just across the corridor from the Billiard Room, which rather cramped our style when we used to have races which involved jumping from bed to bed amid much excited squealing. But that was in the future.

I can't remember being especially homesick that night. I think everything was so strange that I was still taking it all in. Besides, my main occupation was a desperate need to go to the loo after lights out in spite of the fact that we had all queued up and 'been' before bed. I expect it was a nervous reaction to the happenings of the day. But could I remember where it was? It wasn't a pleasant journey along a dimly lit corridor with dark wood panelling and portraits of the Mostyn ancestors glaring down at me. At last I saw a door that was slightly open and the light inside was on. Thank goodness – it was the loo! That was the first of many trips I made that night, clad in my pink winceyette pyjamas and clutching Rabbit for moral support. But it was much more than that – it was the beginning of being able to think for myself and to becoming the independent person I grew up to be.

I can't remember being desperately homesick during the first weeks at school. It was after spending a weekend 'leave-out' with my parents that it dawned on me that this situation was destined to go on for years. It wasn't a happy thought. I didn't cry much but after every leave-out or half-term I used to be violently sick at the thought of the weeks ahead, away from the comfort of my home and family.

Rob told me later that my mother was in an even worse state than me. I'm still mystified as to why they sent me away – not long before he died Rob promised me that it was never his idea – he liked having me at home. I think it was the thing that middle-class parents did in those days, though neither of mine had been away to school. Also, they felt I would enjoy always having kids of my own age around and they were right, but it took me a long time to realise this.

Gloddaeth Hall was not an establishment of academic excellence. Far from it! But there were some subjects that were well taught and they were the ones that I was good at for the rest of my school career. English was one and maths might have been another had I not had such a bad experience at Ardrossen. I developed a great interest in history and geography, largely because of the painting books at the School in the Sun, and I loved singing although I was hopeless at it. But best of all were my private elocution lessons.

I was taught by Miss Musgrave who was very attractive

and came from County Wicklow in the Republic of Ireland. She introduced me to poetry and taught me how to read it aloud, which is something I still enjoy. She also taught me the art of speaking in public and I still do that with initial apprehension but never with fear. I loved her dearly and I wish I could tell her how grateful I am for all she did for me.

Nature walks in the school grounds were also fun and usually ended with somebody falling in the mud or going into too deep water in their wellington boots. I tried hard to be good at hockey and netball, though I never succeeded. I wasn't too bad at tennis and rounders which we played in the summer but, being a plump child and usually trying rather too hard, I was constantly falling over on the gravel netball and tennis courts and grazing my hands and knees. A bad fall usually needed treatment from Sister Hopper, who said to me as she cut a piece of loose skin from my badly grazed hand while I sat biting my lip but unflinching, 'I'll say this for you, Diana, you never make a fuss!'

Praise indeed.

But the highlight of the week was a visit from Mr Davies and his riding school ponies – what joy! He took us out on hacks but he also taught us the rudiments of jumping and what I now realise was basic dressage. His ponies were rather smart and my favourite was a roan with white spots on his bottom. He, unoriginally, was called Snowy and I loved him a lot but not as much as Peggy Pony.

When I was so very homesick during my first term my Mum told me that if I still felt the same by the end of term I needn't go back. She was either a very wise woman or she was taking an enormous gamble but, sure enough, after Christmas I was quite happy to return to join my friends. There was quite a resemblance to Enid Blyton's school stories at times – we did have the odd midnight feast when we could smuggle in food after a leave out and we had plenty of larks in the dorm when Sister was out of earshot.

Two sisters, Diane and Cheryl Morrison, brought their own mattresses to school since the regulation ones were so worn and the bedsprings were so dipped that it was a wonder we didn't all leave suffering from curvature of the spine.

On Sister's night off we used to tip the Morrison sisters out of bed and use their mattresses as trampolines. I remember that, to their credit, they were very generous about it and joined in the fun.

One day – it was February 6 1952 – we were all summoned to the gym, which also served as an assembly hall, and told in solemn tones by Miss Hill, one of the joint headmistresses, that His Majesty King George VI had died early that morning. There was a shocked silence and some girls and teachers cried. We all cheered up though when Miss Hill announced that there would be no lessons that day and we played quiet games or sang suitably sombre songs standing round the old piano played by Miss Campbell, the very pretty games teacher who we all loved. I mention this because it was nearly 70 years ago and such an announcement has not been made since. King George's elder daughter who became Queen Elizabeth II is now over 90 and has reigned over a constantly changing nation with diligence, tact and humour.

My mother, who was intelligent rather than academic, began to realise that most girls left Gloddaeth with very few qualifications and, although she wasn't a pushy parent, she had a bit more ambition for me. After three years I left and went to Queen Ethelburga's School in Harrogate, the Cheltenham of the north.

I was really sad to leave Gloddaeth because I'd made some good friends including two Thai girls (we called them Siamese in those days) who I wrote to for several years. They were the first non-Brits I'd ever met and they gave me a lifelong interest in people of other cultures.

After the initial homesickness, Gloddaeth had been a lot of fun and the best of it was that I'd learned to stand on my own two feet and, although I always loved my home, I never felt that searing homesickness again.

There was one aspect of the school, though, which always puzzled us. The school had two headmistresses. One was small and dainty and had, I think, an Oxbridge degree. She taught English to the seniors. The other taught games and wore a tweed suit, a collar and tie and a Trilby hat. They both lived together in the Oak Parlour. Even at the tender age of nine in an era when no one ever spoke about relationships, we knew there was something not quite usual about this arrangement.

Long afterwards, when I was in my thirties, I read Evelyn Waugh's Decline and Fall about a rather odd private school in Wales, and I laughed all the way through.

*Mum and me on the beach at Llandudno, on
an outing from Gloddaeth Hall*

*Off to yet another new
school in my new suit*

Chapter 13

ALL CHANGE

In September 1954, mum and I were again packing my trunk ready for the autumn term but this time the uniform was brown – new uniform with five inch hems in the hope that everything would last as I grew (it did) and new nametapes on everything – thank goodness for Granny.

My parents had at last cottoned on to the fact that I was not going to discover whatever academic gifts I might have at Gloddaeth Hall and had enrolled me at Queen Ethelburga's School on the outskirts of the Yorkshire spa town of Harrogate – the Cheltenham of the north. As far as I could tell, the main reason for their choice was that the daughter of a friend of theirs had once been there. Even less comprehensible was the fact that Hilary my cousin and constant companion was at a different school in Harrogate and my good friend Julie Banks at yet another.

QE, as it was known, was everything that Gloddaeth

was not. It had been built as a school just before the Great War, so it catered for the needs of 200 girls, divided into four houses with 50 in each. Most of us slept in separate cubicles along a corridor and each cubicle had a bed (with a comfortable mattress), a wardrobe, chest of drawers, dressing table and chair. Every one had a window with a view of the Yorkshire moors – and also of the road along which the soldiers from the nearby army camp marched up and down. We spend a lot of time looking out of our windows …

I was used by this time to communal living but for the majority of girls who had never left home before, the privacy must have helped in the first traumatic days. I, however, felt very lucky (although I would much rather have gone to a day school) and to me QE seemed like a rather luxurious hotel.

For a start the food was good – it was to me anyway. Not everybody thought so – but they should have had a spell at Gloddaeth. We actually had chips once a week for lunch and roast potatoes on a Sunday. We had sausages and bacon for breakfast twice a week and supper was always edible so we didn't go to bed hungry.

As the school buildings were in a long line we had to walk for our meals and it was a long way from my house at the bottom to the dining rooms at the top. All the buildings were linked by a covered way but it didn't offer much cover in the Yorkshire winters and to combat this we all wore cloaks to get from one building to another. These were brown with yellow hoods and warm linings and though we hated the rest of our uniform, we loved our cloaks. I think mine is still in the loft with a lot of other history.

In the middle of the school buildings was the chapel and we spent a lot of time there because QE was a member of the Anglican group of Woodard Foundation schools, dedicated to producing young people well versed in the Christian faith – and we certainly were. The school's rather outlandish name was a symbol of this. Queen Ethelburga was the Christian daughter of King Ethelbert and Queen Bertha of Kent who had been converted by none other than St Augustine in the late sixth century.

Ethelburga travelled north to marry King Edwin of Northumbria, a pagan whom she converted and who was baptised, allegedly, on the spot where York Minster now stands. We had to learn all this in the first few weeks of starting school, along with a lot of other history, and it is forever engraved on my mind.

But back to that first day ...

While I was unpacking my overnight bag and finding a comfortable place for Pooh Bear to sit and survey the scene, my mum was talking to a tall girl with dark, curly hair who had been dropped off early by her parents and seemed glad to have someone for company.

When I went outside to say goodbye to Mum and Rob, Mum said, 'She seems nice. I reckon you two could be good friends.'

Huh! thought my 12 year-old self, I'm old enough to choose my own friends now.

But, as ever, Mum was right and Carole and I were the best of friends from that first day. We shared each other's joys and sorrows, not only at school but for the rest of our lives.

Apart from the lack of freedom, which I never ceased to resent, I quite enjoyed my time at QE. The staff were properly qualified and the teaching was good on average. I never could get on with maths however well I was taught, and for that I still blame Miss Nicholson. The difficulty was ingrained long before Miss Keele, the red haired Irishwoman who first taught my class at QE. Miss Keele would throw pieces of chalk at the uncomprehending ones, then the board rubber. Finally she would get hold of us by the ear and mutter, 'Child o' grace, child o' grace, will ye never understand …'

I never did and the happiest day of my school life was when my mother went to the headmistress to ask if I could drop maths and she agreed.

I loved English and history and geography but I was also quite good at French, Latin, science and art. In fact, I realised that when things were explained to me sufficiently that I was actually quite bright. And I got brighter until I was often top of the class in the fortnightly marks list. This was a surprise and I revelled in it.

Games, however, were a different matter. I could never quite decide whether I really was hopeless or whether I just wanted to be. I never mastered the mysteries of lacrosse and I always opted to play a place at cricket as far away from the main action as possible. Tennis was different – probably because it wasn't a team game – and I really enjoyed it. So much so that I was chosen to play for my house, much to the entertainment of my other non-athletic friends who used to watch me practice with my team and did their best to put me off.

The main entertainment for those of us who had very little interest in sport was to see how long we could hide in the changing room without being discovered by the gamesmistress, Miss Constantine, who had played lacrosse for England. She later confessed that she had known where we were all the time – it was just much less trouble to leave us there.

I wasn't a particularly well-behaved kid in the first few years at school. Very few of us were. Larks after lights-out were the main opportunities for mischief and we were forever being discovered by our head of house or worse, by the housemistress, Miss Snape, who rather seemed to lack a sense of humour.

After I was accused of bad manners in one school report, my mother went to see the headmistress, Miss Kerr, who reassured her that many girls had had far worse reports than mine from Miss Snape. My mum was reassured but not quite satisfied and I got a bit of a roasting from her when we got home. After that I decided I'd better mend my ways or at least not get caught. That was really the beginning of my determination to do as well as I possibly could, and stick to the Hill Standard which was constantly instilled into us at our school on the hill: 'To be the best I can be, being what I am, with the gifts I have got.'

I think of it even now and realise what a good guide to life it was – and still is – and I decided to make the most of the things I was good at. These did not, of course, include maths and games.

What I loved most of all, though, and this had been fostered at Gloddaeth, was reciting poetry, speaking in public, acting in plays – in fact, I was a real show off and I still am. At QE there were endless dramatic opportunities – school plays, house plays, senior plays, junior plays, nativity plays, verse speaking and public speaking competitions, reading the lesson in chapel – and I was always in on everything for which I was eligible. I just loved it and under the tutelage of Penny Noel, our drama teacher, I was able to make the most of this gift I had got.

Penny was young and very pretty but she often seemed sad and we decided she had had an unhappy love affair. It made her even more appealing as a teacher. We loved her even if others hadn't. With her to coach me, I won a poetry competition and the school public speaking competition. No one was more surprised than me and it has stood me in good stead. I still get up to speak in public without getting in a state – and I still enjoy it. Thank you Penny.

The big social event of the school year was the School Birthday, October 21, which (apart from being Trafalgar Day) commemorated the time when a teacher from Queen Margaret's School in York founded QE with just 12 pupils. There were no lessons but there was a service in the chapel – inevitably – and lots of free time, followed by a party in the evening for which we all had new dresses(lots of competition there), ate a slap up supper and then enjoyed an evening of dancing.

The only trouble was that no men were allowed to attend, so, as in Joyce Grenfell's well-known poem, we were 'doing the Dashing White Sergeant, and we danced it bust to bust.'

This activity was pretty daunting as we grew more senior when it was expected that we should dance with Miss Kerr, the headmistress, whose nickname was Tabby due to her fondness for cats. She was particularly well endowed but not very tall so taking the part of the men – which we were expected to – could cause problems on a crowded dance floor.

We ended the evening by singing the school hymn which was entitled LUCE MAGISTRA and its twelve letters represented the twelve girls who had been the first pupils at the school. It was also the school motto and it translated as Light being the Test. Its origins came from a fable in which young eagles were made to stare at the sun and those who couldn't do so without blinking were thrown out of the nest – so light should be our test as it was theirs. But I always felt sorry for those little eaglets who didn't make it.

It was inevitable among groups of rather silly teenage girls that the teachers should be the butt of our juvenile humour. What we failed to realise then was that these women were pioneers in a man's world, pioneers who were following in the footsteps of the suffragettes to create lives for the rest of us where we would no longer be second class citizens but could hold our own with our male counterparts.

Even now, more than 60 years later there's still work to be done but we're very nearly there thanks, to the efforts of the likes of Tabby (MA Cantab) a student of Girton, the first Cambridge college to be opened specifically for women, her second in command, Miss Battersby (Batty) who studied classics at Oxford at the same time as politician Quentin Hogg, later Lord Hailsham, and who made Latin texts come alive for me, and Miss Donkersley (Donkey) who taught us all the wonders of our own language through Shakespeare, Lord Byron and T S Eliot and the other giants of English literature.

They and so many like them toiled to educate the generations of girls in their care so that the day would come when they would all have a qualification and, if they were lucky, a job. They would never be cast on the scrap heap of middle class life like poor Auntie Elsie, whatever happened to them.

By the autumn of 1957 the exams known then as O levels were creeping ever closer. I was taking eight, which was quite a lot in those days, but there was none of the angst surrounding exams as there is today. We were taught the syllabus, we took our 'mocks', we had marks predicted (no grades then) and somehow we took it all in our stride – even if we didn't, there was no counselling and not much advice on exam techniques. We were left to our own devices and somehow we managed. But it was a very different world then and the pressures on us were so much less.

'Just do your best, you can't do more,' said Mum and Rob. And so I did.

We took our exams in the hot summer of 1958. I can remember sitting revising in the library with the smell of recently cut grass and the click of cricket bats outside the window. I was glad it wasn't me playing cricket. Then it was all over and we were free. Not completely free, however, because we still had to finish the school term somehow – no going home as soon as exams were done. We swam (the school had its own slightly mucky pool), played tennis and discussed our plans for the future. I started to knit a scarf which I never finished and unravelled years later when my children needed some wool.

Then it was time to say goodbye to those who weren't coming back, like Lynne who was going into nursing straight from school. But it wasn't really goodbye because Lynne is a friend still and we meet every so often for lunch, together with Barbara, Linda, Joy and Gill and many memories.

Halfway up the Langdale Pike by
Dungeon Ghyll, with childhood friends
Julie and John, and Rob

With Hilary in our jodhpurs as usual. Our jodhpurs were bought to last, and they did!

Chapter 14

A LIFETIME PASSION

I can't remember exactly when my passion for all things equine began but I think it was when my mother read Black Beauty to me. I was six and we were staying with my godparents, Auntie Alice and Uncle Arthur who lived in the old Roman town of Chester. Getting there had been very exciting as we had driven through the Mersey Tunnel, an amazing feat of engineering for those days. Little did I know that before long we'd be driving through that tunnel on my way to the dreaded boarding school Gloddaeth Hall, and it wouldn't be exciting at all – but that was all in the future.

At Auntie Alice's, Mummy and I shared a double bed and we put a bolster down the middle so that we couldn't kick one another (inadvertently) in the night. Black Beauty was my bedtime story – I read quite well for my age but I wasn't quite up to that standard.

From my mother's point of view it turned out to be a

big mistake. I was captivated by the adventures of Beauty, Ginger and Merrylegs and wept bitterly at the fate of poor Ginger. This could have put me off horses for ever but it had exactly the opposite effect and awoke in my small soul a passion which has never left me.

It wasn't until I was eight that I began to learn to ride, though. I had dreamed of doing so ever since that trip to Chester. For my eighth birthday I was given a pair of jodhpurs – stiff cavalry twill with those ridiculous 'elephant ears' sticking out at the sides (whatever purpose did they serve?). The jodhpurs were certainly bought to last as a photograph of me before my first ride shows – they were enormous. And they did last until I was thirteen and my growing legs had taken up the many wrinkles.

I also had a 'hard hat', although it wasn't very hard by today's standards, and a yellow tie with horse heads on it. My lace up Start-Rite school shoes were my only footwear until my next birthday when I was given a smart pair of jodhpur boots. How proud I was of them.

I was collected at our garden gate by Peggy, a lovely lady who was 'walking out' with George Mays whose family had the riding stables. Confusingly, the pony she had brought for me to ride was also called Peggy, so she was always known as Peggy Pony. I fell instantly in love with her and one of the first great traumas of my life was when I finally grew too big for her.

The Mays family were dark skinned and dark eyed and looked as if they had been born on a horse. Way back I think they had probably been gypsies and this was another source of wonder to me and my cousin Hilary who soon joined me on my Sunday morning excursions with the Peggies or often with George. It had to be Sunday in summer because for the rest of the week those ponies gave rides on the beach. I used to feel rather sorry because they had to go out with us on their day off, but it must actually have been a relief to them because, as our riding improved, we used to take them up the beach towards Blackpool and let them gallop back along the long stretch of sand. Stopping was always a bit of a lottery because by this time they were wildly excited and it was lucky that there was a stretch of shingle at the end to slow them down.

Some of the things we did would not have been approved by the Pony Club but, thanks to George and Peggy we developed firm seats and were taught to use our legs rather than pulling constantly on the reins. I've never thought of myself as much of a rider but I knew how to stay on board and I can't remember ever being nervous in those far off days.

One of the things we enjoyed most was to go and help

the Mays to give rides on the beach. The rides cost 6d to walk and 1/- to go a bit further and trot and Hilary and I did most of the walking and trotting. We set off early in the morning with old Mr Mays driving a huge piebald horse called Bill in the flatbed trailer with Mrs Mays beside him and the trailer loaded with everything which would be needed for the day. Riding beside the trailer would be Doris, their unmarried daughter of whom we were a bit afraid (we'd heard some of the words she used to the more awkward horses), and George, both leading several ponies, followed by Hilary and me, rejoicing in our free ride from the stables to our 'stand' on the beach.

And there we would spend the day, running up and down leading unsteady children and often adults – nobody really considered that they might topple off and they wore no safety gear. All the saddles, however, had metal hoops on the front so that those who had never ridden before had something to hang on to and I can't remember accidents ever happening. These hoops were very useful when we were learning to ride but got in the way when going at speed. But none of it mattered to us as long as the saddle was attached to a horse.

Mrs Mays spent the day sitting in front of a piece of canvas which shielded her from the wind. She took the money in a big leather satchel while Mr Mays, George and Doris heaved people up on to the horses and would take the more experienced for a spin on the sands while we continued our leading up and down. At lunchtime we ate our sandwiches, which by this time were usually full of sand as there was nearly always a wind blowing. Then more running up and down.

We didn't pack up until we saw that the rival outfits, the Millers and Rimmers, were getting ready to go – no point in losing valuable business. Then we got all the horses and ponies ready for the return journey, climbed aboard our various modes of transport and returned to the stables.

This wasn't the end of the day, however, the ponies had to be unsaddled, fed and led to their various fields. Then more excitement as we were allowed to ride bareback and lead another pony to the field nearest to where I lived. We then walked home still enthusing about the marvellous day we'd had. My mother, who had never had any dealings with horses, was totally mystified.

Of course, for Hilary and me, our greatest wish was to own ponies of our own but it was never going to happen. We lived in a town, albeit it with countryside around us, and we were both at boarding school, but nothing could stop us wishing.

We read all the books written for horse-mad little girls like us, we took out subscriptions to Riding and Pony magazines and did all the competitions in the hope of winning a pony or at least a piece of pony equipment we could use on our riding school friends. We followed avidly the career of a Gloucestershire girl called Pat Smythe who, with few funds but a lot of determination, was carving out a career for herself in the male dominated sport of show jumping – all the way to the Olympic Games.

I had a special spot on my bedroom wall for the pictures of her that I cut out of newspapers and magazines. I had no inkling that, decades later, she and I would become friends and judge tiny Cotswold pony shows together.

We joined the Pony Club and hung about at rallies hoping that someone – anyone – might offer us a ride, but they never did. That had a lasting impact on my life and I vowed that if ever I did have a pony (I still hoped) I would always be happy to lend it to someone less lucky than me. I did and I have.

Meantime, things took a rather miserable turn. The Mays decided to give up the stables which were just not making enough money to keep the whole family, and the ponies were sold or went to good homes. Hilary and I were inconsolable for a while but the Mays, who had always regarded us as family (not surprising since we spent such a lot of time with them) resolved to keep a pony called Georgie who they had rescued from a very cruel home, as it seemed unfair to move him on again.

They said he was ours to ride whenever we liked so we spent many happy hours, one on Georgie and one on a bike. He wasn't an easy ride because he really had a mind of his own and didn't much like stopping when asked but he taught us a lot and we had endless fun with him.

We persuaded Rob to come out with us one day – he had done quite a lot of riding in his youth and had some very smart kit – but it wasn't the greatest success. Proceeding happily along the Promenade on the way to the beach, Georgie decided to inspect one of the many old people's homes along the way. In spite of Rob's protests he took him into the garden and peered through the window of the residents' lounge to the great excitement of the old people. He refused to move until he had seen all he needed and then sauntered off down the path. It was lucky that Rob was such a patient and good humoured man but we couldn't get him to have another go – goodness knows where he and Georgie might have ended up.

The start of sand yachting on the beach – sand yachts were a bit like large go-karts with big sails – restricted our riding activities because horses made it clear that these monsters were the scariest thing they had ever seen. And inevitably, boys eventually came into our lives and took the place of horses for a while – I even had a boyfriend with a sand yacht and it was good fun – but not for ever.

When I settled in the Cotswolds with my husband and two little children, I met one of our neighbours, a delightful lady called Veronica Demuth who had more horses and ponies than she could quite deal with when her daughters were at school and university. Whenever I could I rode her ponies and helped her out with the foals that she bred. My passion was reawakened and this time it was never laid to rest.

This book is meant to be about my childhood but I just need to tell you that since the age of 30 when I bought my first pony (so that I could keep up with my little children who already had one of their own – that's my excuse, anyway) I have never been without ponies and, together with my family, they have been the great joy of my life.

I should be quite rich if it wasn't for them but what is wealth compared with the pleasure that each one has given me? I gave up riding a few years ago when Charlie, the pony love of my life who I had had for 25 years, was put down at the ripe old age of 34. I miss both him and riding dreadfully but I still have three retired ponies in my care. And, although on winter mornings I sometimes wish I wasn't mucking out stables and carrying hay to muddy fields, I can't part with them, I just can't.

POSTCRIPT:

When my husband and I were staying with Hilary a few years before she sadly died, she greeted me with great excitement, saying, 'Di, I've found George Mays – he's living just near the old stables!'

When we knocked on the door we were greeted by a little wizened old man who was unmistakeably George. A grin spread over his face. 'Ee,' he said, 'It's 'iIary – and Di too! Come in, come in!'

In his immaculate sitting room, surrounded by reminders of the past, we drank tea and talked about old times, which he remembered as well as we did. He and I discussed the rising price of hay and the farrier and I told him about our ponies and what we got up to with them.

He was by then over 90 and had only recently given up helping with donkey rides on the beach. As we chatted, six decades melted away and Hilary and I were twelve and ten again ...

Some people you never forget and George was one of them.

Going out for a ride on Peggy, my first pony love

With Georgie on the beach.
Where is my riding hat?

*With the Airey family, 'competing' in one of
our home-made gymkhanas.
Left to right: Carol, Heather, me and Peter*

Chapter 15

GIRLS AND BOYS COME OUT TO PLAY

We had a lot more fun when I was a kid – that's not an original thought, I know, but we really did. There were very few manufactured games and toys but we made our own fun. We could do this because, compared to today, there was very little parental supervision.

From quite an early age we roamed around in little gangs, climbing trees (and in my case often falling out of them), making dens and trying to cook (usually potatoes) on very smoky fires. As we grew older we ventured further afield to the beach which was about a mile away. There was never any fear of us drowning as this was an estuary and we seldom saw the sea at close quarters. Besides, the tide had an annoying habit of coming in (and going out) when we weren't there. But we had fun fishing for shrimps in the warm little pools under the pier and, of course, building sand castles which were never there when we went back to find them.

Our parents had forbidden us to go into the sandhills because, they said, 'very peculiar people' lurked in there – and we never did because we had seen some of those people creeping out. Instead we played 'chicken' on the railway line which ran close to the sea front. This was nothing like so hazardous as it sounds because the line wasn't electrified then and in any case, the ground was so flat that we could see the train coming for miles.

Much more dangerous was playing 'flying' which we did at a friend's house as late in the day as we could stay out because it needed to be going dark to have the desired effect.

Carol, Heather, Peter, John and I would go round to the Johnson's house (no relation to my Johnson cousins) ostensibly to 'play' with the two girls, Pippa and Penny. We would tell Penny, who was much younger than us, that we were going flying that evening and persuade her to stay in her bedroom until we returned from our flight.

First, we went to the window of their parents' bedroom and called to the fairies to bring us some wings. Then, with Penny safely shut away, we jumped out of the window on to a ledge below and made our way precariously along another ledge, over a rustic arch adorned with very prickly roses and jumped to the ground. Then we rushed in to tell Penny about our adventures. How we never got caught or had dreadful falls I'll never know – and our parents never knew a thing about it. What did they think we were doing, I wonder?

There were several entertainments, though, which did involve grown ups. One of these was a trip to the market in Lytham in John's grandfather's pony and trap. This was great fun but what intrigued me most was some of the names which 'Granfer' Redfern called his pony.

I repeated them during lunch after my first trip and was a bit surprised to see my mother, granny and grandpa and uncle (who came to lunch from his office nearly every day) desperately trying not laugh. Mum advised me later that it wouldn't be a good idea to use those words again. But she didn't stop me going back.

Much more respectable were my visits with Grandpa to hear the orchestra playing at the end of St Annes pier. Nearly every seaside town had a pier in those days and there were three at nearby Blackpool. I loved sitting by Grandpa listening to the music and developed a crush on the first violinist whose name, I still remember, was Diana Inglis.

At the end Grandpa would buy us a delicious ice cream from the van at the entrance to the pier. When I was quite a lot older I made friends with a girl called Gilli Freeman whose grandfather owned the Central Pier in Blackpool. He would give us complimentary tickets to some of the matinees and we saw what must have been very early performances by rising stars like Morcambe and Wise and Ken Dodd.

I'm ashamed to say that we didn't think they were very funny. Perhaps they improved as they got more experience – all of them make me laugh a lot when I see old clips of them now.

Although Blackpool wasn't the most gentile of places even then, it was exciting to live nearby. Our twice yearly visits to the Tower Circus were greatly looked forward to. It was marvellously spectacular and included acts which involved elephants, lions, tigers and often sea lions which I couldn't bear to watch today. I particularly loved the dancing Liberty Horses and their handlers, all in sparkly costumes, and the antics of the clowns Charlie Careoli and his sidekick, Paul.

In the final scene we always waited in anticipation as the floor went down, the sea came in, the lighting was even more spectacular and acrobats, usually dressed as mermaids, would perform above the water and sometimes in it, often accompanied by sea lions. It was another world and we came away with stars in our eyes.

Less fun and very smelly were visits to Blackpool Zoo which was positioned under the Tower. Wild animals paced round their cages or simply slept their miserable lives away in dark corners. How could we ever have thought of it as entertainment? I do actually remember feeling very uncomfortable at the zoo and I think my mother did too because we didn't go there very often.

What did happen every year was our visit to Blackpool Illuminations. T'lights, as they were known locally, were revived in the late 40s, after being extinguished for the duration of the war. It was so exciting to stay up until it was really dark and then drive, usually with my mother and granny and sometimes one of the cousins, along the Golden Mile.

Mum had to drive at a snail's pace as everyone in the world seemed to be queuing to see them too but that was all part of the fun because it gave us longer to feast our eyes on the fairyland all around us. Not long ago my cousin Martin took us on a trip to see t'lights and they had lost very little of their magic after more than half a century. To eat fish and chips at the end of the visit was the icing on the cake.

One of the best things about living near Blackpool as we were growing up was that the stars who were performing in the town during the season usually preferred to rent homes in swanky St Annes to get away from the crowds and the bright lights. Some, like comedians Al Read and George Formby, lived permanently in the town but one summer we had Terry Thomas living next door but one to us and on another occasion Adam Faith rented a house just up the road. There was always a gaggle of fans outside his gate and how the owners cleaned the slogans off the gateposts after he left I can't imagine.

Down in the town you never knew who you were going to be queuing behind in a shop or at the next table in a café. Would it be comedian Bob Monkhouse or actor Robert Morley? To name only two.

Visits to the circus, the zoo and the very glitzy pantomime (which also featured a famous star) were always with our parents but from our very early teens Hilary and I (when we weren't riding on the beach) were allowed to go to the cinema in Blackpool completely on our own.

Blackpool had a reputation as a sinful place and a refuge for criminals even then, but nobody stopped us going.

Our outings involved Hilary catching the bus near her house, me getting on much later at the stop near mine, changing in St Annes square and then chugging along to Blackpool to swoon over Dirk Bogarde, Cary Grant,

Gregory Peck and all the other handsome stars. But Dirk was always our favourite. Then we'd catch the bus again around ten o'clock and go home, changing again and each walking home on our own from the bus stop. If our parents were anxious they never showed it and nothing untoward ever happened to us.

As we grew a bit older, most of us in our very middle class community went to boarding school. My school friends often complained about being lonely in the holidays but we weren't because we went to The Dancing Class. This took place several times during the Christmas and Easter holidays. It was run by Miss Ashcroft and Miss Brown, both of whom had taught our parents to dance – people didn't move around much in those days and most of my friends were the children of my parents' friends.

I had not inherited the musical instincts of most of the rest of my family and I had very little sense of rhythm which was a bit of a handicap when learning to dance. This meant that, as I struggled, I was usually seized by one of the teachers who made great efforts to teach me how to dance the waltz, the quickstep and the foxtrot without getting my feet in a muddle or treading on my partner's toes.

Usually it was Miss Brown who, I discovered, was corseted in whalebone from armpit to thigh. My mother said she had worn those corsets (or their equivalent) even in her day. To be fair, she had an excellent figure in what must have now been her seventies. I learnt to dance pretty quickly then, largely to get rid of the embarrassment of dancing with the teacher. I soon learnt the waltz, loved the intricacies of the quickstep but I never mastered the foxtrot. Not that it really mattered because I can never remember being asked to dance any of them in public.

Miss Ashcroft and Miss Brown also moved with the times and taught us the samba, the rhumba, the cha-cha, which had just become fashionable, and the rudiments of jive and rock 'roll. They were pretty switched on, those two.

All through my life when I've seen others struggling on the dance floor, I've been grateful to them for teaching me one of the social graces I've never forgotten.

But the dancing class was also a meeting place for shy teenagers who could get to know the opposite sex without having to be introduced by one's parents (honestly, that's what happened in those days) – a very embarrassing experience. We also had Dances during those holidays. These were rather staid affairs in a local hotel with lots of parents in attendance. What we failed to recognise at the time was that, but for those parents, we'd have had very few friends.

The most energetic parent of all was Auntie Edna. She

wasn't an auntie at all but kids always called other people's parents who they knew well 'auntie' and 'uncle.' She was married to Uncle Max and they had three children, Anne, who I had got to know at primary school, and her two little brothers, Peter and Jimmy.

The other member of the family was Auntie Maisie, who was Edna's sister. She was large and formidable until you got to know her. She was matron of a large hospital in Worcester – and she looked it. She spent her holidays with the family and, although she caused much amusement by forgetting that she wasn't 'Matron' in the family environment, we were all very fond of her.

Auntie Edna was about half the size of her sister and she had the most twinkling eyes of anyone I have ever known. She also had the most dreadful stammer which took a bit of getting used to. She would tell us some of the funniest stories but when she got stuck on a word she would never let us help her out but would slap her knee until the word came. It was said that she only stammered after a bad fall from a horse – she loved horses as much as I did. And that was the cause of the only quarrel I had with Anne, who was one of my best friends and still is, seventy years later. Anne had been given a pony by her parents but she wouldn't ride it …Imagine how I felt! I who wanted a pony more than anything else in the world. Anyway, we never let it come between us.

As well as organising dances for us, with a group of other parents, Auntie Edna would invite at least ten of us to a picnic tea in the garden every Sunday in the summer holidays so that we didn't lose touch with one another. It sounds very tame now but it was good fun and pretty wild and noisy.

I remember Bill Dawson, my boyfriend of the time, giving rides round the garden (which was quite big) on his moped – at full throttle. Most of us got tossed off into the bushes. I just loved these noisy occasions and being at Edna's house generally, but Anne, bless her, adored the time she spent at my house where all was quiet and tranquil.

The family nicknamed me Miss Dunket – no one knew why – and that's what those who are still alive call me even now.

Having spent endless hours with Hilary, mostly riding or messing about with ponies, it was now Cousin Martin and I who spent more time together, mostly listening to pop music – rock 'n roll was in full swing and the music of a certain group of cheery Liverpudlians was starting to take the country by storm.

A chap called Don kept a record shop in downtown St Annes and we spent some happy hours crammed into a soundproof cubicle in the shop, sometimes with other friends, listening to all the latest hits. I don't remember ever buying anything but Don didn't seem to mind.

As an only child, I actually spent quite a lot of time on my own and I liked it this way because I could indulge in my other favourite hobby (as well as horses) which was reading. How I loved to be transported to other places with other people (who became my good friends) and be lost in their world for hours.

I learnt to read quite early thanks to all the reading aloud done by my family and I never went to bed without a story. My first efforts on my own were books that had been my bedtime stories – all the Beatrix Potter books, Alison Uttley's tales of Squirrel, Hare and Little Grey Rabbit and, inevitably, Enid Blyton whose stories of children having the most amazing adventures kept me enthralled for hours.

The Famous Five, the Secret Seven, the girls at Mallory Towers – they all became my friends and I couldn't live without them. I never liked Little Noddy, though, I simply couldn't see the point of him. Then there were the horsey stories, mainly by the three Pullein-Thompson sisters, Josephine, Diana and Christine. The fact that the heroine of the story always got her pony in the end, filled me with (unfulfilled) hope.

My special reading place was on a stair, at the point where our stairs bent round and where I was just out of sight of anyone who called at the house. Much as I loved having visitors, I never wanted to be interrupted when I was reading. The stair was still my reading refuge as I progressed to Arthur Ransome, then Jane Austen, the Brontes and later to Nancy Mitford and Evelyn Waugh. What adventures I had with them all.

So, being a kid and then a teenager all those years ago, might seem very odd to todays kids, but I shall always remember it as the very best of times.

With Julie on top of Harrison Stickle on
Langdale Pike

Rowing on Lake Windermere

Chapter 16

HOLIDAYS BACK IN THE DAY

When I was a kid, holidays were far from being the exotic affairs they are today. Very few people crossed the Atlantic to America, or ventured (unless they had previously served the Empire) into the unknown lands east of Istanbul – or Constantinople as it was known in those days.

You had to be pretty well-heeled to spend indolent summers in the south of France. In any case, the rumours about French plumbing were not encouraging and very few people were tempted to visit Germany so soon after the end of the war. If you did decide to go abroad or to the Continent, it was usually to Switzerland or Scandinavia where the plumbing was a lot better than ours and where there was no distressing war damage on account of those countries remaining neutral during the conflict.

Although we were not hard up, we certainly didn't have money to throw away on a few days in the sun –

though we might have had if I'd been allowed to go to a day school. In any case, the grandparents were getting older and my mother, who seemed to take responsibility for all of them, never wanted to be too far away in case they were taken ill and we had to come rushing back. They never were, but we had some splendid holidays within the confines of the UK and never felt deprived that we weren't swanning off to somewhere more exotic.

Because we lived by the sea – although we didn't see it much on account of it being an estuary where the tide seemed to be out much more than it was in – we seldom had holidays by the sea. The one exception in the early days was to Devon where Step-Granny, bizarrely, owned part of the pier at Teignmouth, near the very popular holiday resort of Torquay.

It was left to her by her late husband and Rob had the rather unenviable job of being its company secretary which meant that he had to work on the accounts each day while we had a holiday. Not much fun for him, as he counted the takings from 'What the Butler Saw' and other innocuous slot machines but, as ever, he never complained.

The journey must have been a nightmare for my parents on account of my propensity to vomit during a car journey, short or long, and so the journeys always took ages and involved an overnight stay at a suitable halfway stage. This was nearly always the Cotswolds – little did I know then that this area would eventually be my home.

'You'll find Devon very different from Lancashire,' said my mum. 'It's much warmer – there are palm trees growing there and lots of flowers we never see here. And the soil is red and so are the cows but the sea is bright turquoise blue when the sun shines.'

And so it was and it was very exciting once we got there, but even then I was developing a love of the craggy uplands, the rushing streams and the cold, still lakes of the land I still regard as my second home – The Lake District.

This was lucky, really, because the Devon trips were soon abandoned as a family holiday – I think the vomiting had worn down even Rob's patience – and we went to the Lake District or to the Fells, sometimes even venturing into Scotland, all of which could reached in far less time from our Lancashire home.

Usually we took one of the cousins with us – it was Hilary in the early days, and later Martin when he and I enjoyed holidays with a bit more going on.

We went to three different places which all held delights for us. The smartest was the Langdale Chase Hotel where the gardens, full of hydrangeas in the summer, sloped down to the shores of Lake Windermere. One of the things which fascinated me from a very young age was that all the crockery and cutlery had a little squirrel stamped on it. Of course, these were red squirrels then, like Beatrix Potter's mischievous Squirrel Nutkin – the grey variety had not arrived in great numbers to the detriment of the red just yet.

Langdale Chase was run by Mrs Dalzell and her daughter Dorothy, who liked a drop of gin but never let it interfere with her treatment of her guests, none of whom she ever forgot. I rather wished she had when Brian, my first husband, and I went there on our honeymoon and she recognised me instantly. She promised not to tell anyone else but she must have 'forgotten' because, when we left, all the staff came to say goodbye and made us promise to remember them to my mother …

During those childhood holidays, the thing we loved best was the fact that the hotel had a boathouse and two rowing boats which had seen better days. Rob taught us to row on the lake and we always had a lot of fun, but our real ambition was to row across the lake, which we had been strictly been forbidden to do but which didn't look very far.

One morning, when mum and Rob weren't about, we

collected Jeremy, a boy we had made friends with, and legged it down to the boathouse. We pushed out the first boat and jumped in. It was a beautiful sunny day and as we skimmed across the still water we felt just as though we were either the Swallows or the Amazons.

What we didn't know was that mum had been looking from her bedroom window through Rob's binoculars at the beautiful view of the lake on this magical morning when she suddenly spotted us just about to reach the other side. Not only that, but the skies darkened and the rain came down as it only can in the Lake District and there were her only daughter, her only niece and somebody else's son stranded on the far side of the lake.

Luckily, just as she and Rob were wondering who they could sent to rescue us, the rain stopped, the sun came out again and she saw us climb back into the boat and make for the near shore. She never let us out of her sights.

We arrived back feeling very pleased with ourselves – until mum appeared. I had never seen her so cross and I never did again. Of course, I later realised, when I had children of my own, that she had felt absolutely terrified for us and very responsible for not realising what we were up to. The atmosphere for the rest of the day was pretty icy – even Rob wasn't taking our part for once – but they soon thawed out and we never did anything like that again … at least not within the sight of any grown ups.

We did a lot of walking and exploring in the Lakes but the highlight of all the holidays we had there was when we climbed the Langdale Pikes – this time with Rob in charge.

It was a stiff climb, even for relatively fit teenagers, but it was so worth it and the view from the top of the first Pike, Harrison Stickle, was breathtaking. It seemed that the whole of the Lake District was spread out before us, just as Wordsworth and his pals had seen it.

We had walked through sunshine and cold rain (even on a warm summer day) to get there, but as we reached the summit the sun came out to reveal a landscape that lives with me still.

I have climbed the Pikes several times since then, but nothing compares to that first adventure. I wrote about when I got back to school and my efforts were chosen to appear in the school magazine – my first ever published piece of writing.

Our other favourite holidays were with Mrs Johnson or Mrs Baines. Mrs Johnson ran Hodge Hill, a family farmhouse on remote Cartmell Fell in Cumbria, where she made every guest enormously welcome and cooked the most delicious and gigantic meals. Full English breakfast was later followed by lunch which was a proper 'dinner' not a snack. If we were in at teatime, a trolley appeared laden with home made scones and cakes and in the evening there was a three course supper …

It was all far too much but, as we all had healthy appetites we just about managed, which was lucky because jolly Mrs Johnson got a bit offended if we left much. One evening, even Step-Granny, who probably had the best appetite of us all, was absolutely defeated. She didn't dare leave anything on her plate so, while Rob kept watch at one door and I guarded the other, Step-Granny nipped into the sitting room and put what she had left on the fire. Then we had to hope that it was consumed by the flames before our heinous crime was discovered.

I once woke up in the night feeling really sick from eating too much rich food and when my mum came to see what was wrong, I groaned, 'All I can think of is pork and cream.' This then became a family joke for anyone who had overeaten.

What Hilary and I loved best about Hodge Hill was the fact that there was no electricity. The downstairs was lit by Calor gas but, when we went to bed we took oil lamps with us as there was no gas supply upstairs. Going to sleep with the gentle light flickering on the window sill was very soothing but it was a luxury that today's children would be denied. Health and Safety regulations put a stop to that sort of danger a long time ago.

The Johnson's milking parlour was more modern than the house and a generator powered the milking machine. Every morning we woke to its gentle rhythm and peeped out of the tiny casement windows to see the big black and white beasts making their stately way back to their field in the early morning mist.

I hadn't realised quite how attached Rob had been to Hodge Hill and its surroundings until a few days before he died. I was sitting by his hospital bed with my husband, Malcolm, who loved him as much as I did, when Rob said, 'I've been thinking about my funeral. Don't go lugging bodies about – have me cremated and scatter some of my ashes on Mum's grave and the rest in the graveyard of the little church on Cartmell Fell. Then go and have a slap up weekend at Hodge Hill as a present from me.'

And that's exactly what we did.

I can't remember the name of Mrs Baines' farm but it was on the outskirts of Kirkby Lonsdale on the borders of Lancashire with Westmoreland. The food there was excellent too but, luckily, not quite so generous, as Hilary and I were by now a bit more figure conscious. Mrs Baines had some very friendly pigs in her orchard. Every time they spotted us, they would come snorting towards us – not for food but to have their backs scratched. We grew very fond of those pigs but not as fond as of the ponies we discovered in the village.

These ponies belonged to a man called Jonty Wilson who was something of a national celebrity. His claim to fame was that he had ridden the Roman roads of England with a rather extraordinary television personality of the day, whose name was Nancy Spain, and the journalist and travel writer J H B Peel.

Hilary and I weren't very interested in his celebrity status but we were very keen on his ponies on which we had a lot of fun. They were pretty wild because I don't think they were ridden very much but this just added to the excitement. And as we took our riding hats and boots on every holiday, just in case, we were ready for every eventuality. That was lucky because there were plenty of eventualities and these included swimming the ponies across to the island where they grazed, in the middle of the river Lune.

Many years later I was in a pub called the Old New Inn in the Cotswold village of Bourton-on-the-Water on the Fosse Way. On the wall of the main bar was a series of photographs of none other than Jonty with Nancy Spain and Mr Peel, the journalist.

Scotland, for us, wasn't too long a journey unless one was going to the far north, which we never did (too many opportunities for travel-sickness, I expect). I have to say that one of the best holidays I ever had there had nothing to do with the magnificent scenery or the mysterious lochs, but with the manmade delights of Crieff Hydro which was some way west of Perth.

There were a lot of hydros about then but they have now largely been replaced by spa hotels and all that goes with them to pander to those seeking a more healthy lifestyle. There wasn't too much that was healthy about Crieff Hydro by the time we got there, unless you count drinking large quantities of alcohol.

It wasn't meant to be like that. The hotel had been built around the turn of the twentieth century for the families of the clergy to have holidays they could afford. It was strictly temperance and there was no bar even when we went there in the late 1950s. There was, however, no ruling about bringing in alcohol and drinking it in the bedrooms and the result was that every night, when the wild sessions of Scottish dancing were over, the ground floor of the hotel emptied and all the guests went upstairs for a wee dram or much more and the drinking went on until the early hours and often beyond.

I went one year just with Uncle Joey and Martin and we had a ball. Auntie Stella and Hilary had gone on a music holiday and I loved seeing my usually staid, pillar-of-the-community uncle really let his hair down. We took plenty of healthy exercise in the daytime – there were facilities for tennis, badminton, table tennis, croquet, golf – and lots of other teenagers for us to join up with but every evening it was party time.

Actually, we didn't drink a lot of alcohol – most of us were too young to buy it, although I certainly couldn't vouch for Uncle Joey – but we hardly went to bed. When I got home after two weeks of revelry my mother said, 'You look terrible …' and by that time I felt terrible too – but not regretful in any way.

The last two holidays I had before leaving school were with Auntie Edna and her family in the (then) little seaside village of Saundersfoot on the beautiful Gower Peninsular, often known as 'the little England beyond Wales'. The Manleys had rented a flat in the village. It was a bit of a squash with Edna and Max, the two little boys Peter and Jimmy, Anne and me and the Bun Dog, their large and bouncing Dalmation. And even more so when we were joined by Auntie Maisie who was very large indeed.

When we got there we found that the lavatory wasn't working but somehow we just laughed – it was like that when Edna was around. I think Max must have dealt with it. Meanwhile, we used the garden.

Maisie was also a source of great amusement, both

conscious and unconscious. When she arrived she announced that she was slimming and wouldn't eat breakfast. She didn't and we were all very admiring – until she was spotted at Coles' Corner Café in the village, tucking into a huge knickerbocker glory (lots of fruit but even more ice cream and cream) for her elevenses.

She proved very useful, though, in restraining the Bun Dog who proved rather a nuisance on the beach. When the Bun Dog had satisfied herself that there was absolutely nothing left of our picnic, she would go off after other people's – it didn't make us very popular with neighbouring picnickers. So we tied her to Auntie's deck chair and there she had to stay till Auntie was ready to move – usually to get more ice creams – for all of us this time.

We had a lot of fun playing cricket – the boys were much better than us – on the beach and swimming in a sea which obligingly came in far enough and was deep enough for us to swim properly. We loved it.

A word here about 'wild swimming' which is so fashionable today. People boast now about doing it but we never did anything else. We had two local swimming pools at home but, after Martin's polio which it was suspected he'd picked up there, we didn't go. But every piece of water I ever saw, I was in it without a second thought. Lakes, rivers, streams, tiny pools, in I plunged, often coming home soaking wet or in someone else's borrowed clothes. It didn't make me a good swimmer but I had a lot of fun.

Chapter 17

BIG CHEESE

Going back to school became harder as I got older because there were so many better things to do at home. But when I reached the dizzy heights of the sixth form there were a few, though not many, compensations which would count as very tame today.

We were, for instance, allowed to go into Harrogate on Saturday afternoons unless we were playing in a match (no fear of that on my part). There was no need anymore invent imaginary needy relations whose birthdays we had forgotten and who would be devastated if they didn't receive a card from us.

We had to take a taxi there and back, which was expensive but possible if there were several of us. Often we went to the cinema which was somewhat problematic as the film never ended until we were due back at school. We were required to sweet talk the taxi driver to take us to a deserted entrance round the back.

If we didn't go to the cinema, we spent the afternoon looking longingly at the fashions in Harrogate's very smart shops and buying food, which no longer had to be smuggled in. We also spent time eating huge cream cakes at one of the two tea shops in the town – Hammond Mann's where food was hauled up from the basement kitchen on an extraordinary contraption called a dumbwaiter by waitresses who looked far too old and frail for the job, and Betty's where the choice was greater, but where the cakes weren't quite so exotic.

Betty's is still part of the Harrogate scene but Hammond Mann's, sadly, is no more. Perhaps the modern generation of waiting staff took exception to the dumbwaiter.

Lessons were so much more enjoyable because we now chose to study A levels from the subjects we were good at. I had chosen English, History and Latin – this last wouldn't have been the choice of many but I really liked it. Compared with English and History, Latin was very disciplined and I enjoyed wrestling with the translations of the ancient writers. Added to which Batty, who had taught me ever since I arrived at QE, was delighted now to have students who were keen to learn and do well and, as there were only three of us, this wasn't a difficult task. I grew to like and respect her a lot.

English and history were no problem – my love of them was inherited from my family – and I also took French literature for a year and became quite adept at translating the French classics. Sadly, I've lost that skill, along with most of the Latin, which is now confined to making sense of quotations on gravestones.

But although it was now so much more pleasurable, there was an awful lot to do. No more learning by rote – we really had to think hard now and be selective about what we learned. A levels were much more akin to university exams, as I was later to discover.

Meantime, we were now allowed to bring bikes back to school. This was a mixed blessing when tackling the hills around Harrogate on a sit-up-and-beg Raleigh shopping model with no gears but it was freedom of a sort and we revelled in it. Best of all, I had now become something of an embarrassment on the lacrosse pitch (due to all those hours spent hiding in the changing room) and was asked by Miss Constantine if I would like to go for a bike ride instead of games. She didn't have to ask twice and I had endless fun exploring some of the little villages not far from the school.

The first year in the sixth form was very carefree, once we had got used to the workload. We had very little responsibility and important exams seemed a long way in the future. I was able to hone my dramatic skills, such as they were, and I was really delighted to be awarded 'colours' for Diction for which I was entitled to wear a little blue badge with a gold D.

Similar badges were awarded for such things as music, games, gymnastics and deportment. Needless to say, I wasn't in the running for any of them but I really treasured my diction colours.

I think what had clinched this was my performance as Alfred Doolittle, Eliza's rather embarrassing dustman father, in the previous year's production of Bernard Shaw's Pygmalion. It was a part later immortalised by Stanley Holloway in My Fair Lady, the musical version which took London by storm.

With my face blackened, a blanket tied round my body to make me fatter (this was a welcome change – I'd lost most of my 'puppy fat' as it was then called), ghastly old trousers and jacket and a cap turned back to front, I'd learned to speak the rudiments of cockney from Penny, our diction teacher, and was so heavily disguised that even my Mum didn't recognise me. Apart from the fact that it was midsummer and my outfit was uncomfortably hot, I enjoyed every minute of it.

One thing I particularly remember about that production was that we were actually allowed to swear, as it was part of the script, and Eliza was able to proclaim the immortal words, 'Not bloody likely! I'm going home in a taxi.' How daring we were.

The stage was then my first love but writing came a close second and I was determined to win the school's most prestigious award for literature. It was called the Hugh Bright Essay Prize. I can't remember now who Hugh Bright was – probably a man of the cloth – and I can't recall what I wrote about but I did win it!

My reward was a set of Dickens' novels and my name in gold lettering on the board of past prize winners. The books are still in my bookcase but where the notice board now is I have no idea, since the school moved to another site years ago. Maybe I'll go there one day and have a look.

Of course, aged 17, I couldn't see what was staring me in the face. Being good at acting at school was one thing, trying to make a career of it was another. I was determined to study it at university. Why didn't I realise at the time that writing not acting was really the gift I had been blessed with, and that words would eventually become my career and my lifelong passion?

But this dilemma was a long way in the future. I still had another year at school, this time in the upper sixth, and responsibilities loomed ahead. The list of girls in high places had been posted and, for the first time in my life,

I was one of them. The announcement that I was to be head of my house wasn't a great surprise as there really wasn't anyone else in the running, but to be made deputy head of the whole school was something else and my main feeling was a sense of relief that I hadn't been made head girl – the real Big Cheese. Even so, I was determined to take my new positions seriously and to do the best I could.

As it turned out, being head of my house was the most responsible position. The people in charge of us had changed – Miss Snape had been appointed headmistress of a big girls' grammar school in Leeds and Miss Brown, the house matron, always known as Bruno, had finally retired. Dear Bruno, what a character she was. Woe betide anyone who went to her for the removal of a splinter – we were always getting splinters through running barefoot on the wooden floors, a practice strictly forbidden but assiduously ignored. But under Bruno's 'supervision' we were lucky if she stuck her huge darning needle in the right foot, let alone the right toe. If we went to her feeling ill she would take our temperature though what she could see on her thermometer was questionable. It really didn't matter either way, because her cure for everything was a good dose of quinine. But we all remained pretty healthy and Bruno was a kind and caring woman for whom we felt great affection in spite of her lack of medical skill.

Miss Snape was replaced by Miss Holroyd, who taught biology. She was always known as Wee Holy because she was very small and quiet, to distinguish her from the French teacher, also Miss Holroyd, who was large and rather flamboyant. She was called Dam Holy, short for Madame Holroyd.

As well as her small stature, Wee Holy had rather a little voice which wasn't great for her when trying to get noisy girls in echoing corridors to listen to her. I was not similarly challenged and during my time as head of house I did a lot of her shouting for her. Wee Holy looked as if she had just stepped out of a novel by Jane Austen or Charlotte Bronte – she wore her plaited hair in 'earphones' coiled on either side of her head and on the rare occasions when we had fire practice in the very early morning she would appear with the plaits hanging down her back – they really were very long.

Her subject was biology and, cruel kids that we were, we used to long for the moment when she taught reproduction - first that of the house fly and then the rabbit which was more akin to our idea of the subject. She used to go red all the way up her neck and the redder she got, the more we giggled – I can hardly bare to think if it now – how could we have been so horrible?

During my time as head of house (perhaps to try to amend for past behaviour) I rather took her under my wing, instead of the other way round. I also grew to like and respect her enormously and we had many conversations in her cosy sitting room when I went to say goodnight to her, as we all had to do every night. It helped that her much loved cat, Charlotte, used to come to sit on my knee – and, as so often happened in my life, she really liked my mother.

I found Bruno's replacement, Mrs Whitely, less easy to get on with. She was undoubtedly a much more competent nurse, but she was a bit spikey and the only quinine which she administered was from her Indian tonic bottle, poured into her glass of gin, usually in the company of the extremely eccentric Miss Warner who was deputy house mistress.

One of the perks of being in the upper sixth – though we didn't consider it so at the time – was to have supper with Tabby in the head mistress's house on the occasions when a visiting preacher came to take the service in the school chapel. Most of the preachers were deadly dull and often rather deaf but we loved when it the Dean of York, the Very Revd Eric Milner White, came to supper.

The Dean was rotund and jolly and always seemed to enjoy talking to us – he preached interesting sermons too, which made a change. He was also head of the School Chapter, which consisted mainly of unknown people with double-barrelled names. We had no idea what the Chapter did but we were glad to know that he was in charge of it.

I discovered only recently, when we celebrated the centenary of the end of the Great War that Eric Milner White was a very well known man in church circles. As an army chaplain, he was much decorated for his bravery and his main claim to fame, as a graduate of King's College, Cambridge, was that he first conceived the idea of the Festival of the Nine Lessons and Carols which is now broadcast all over the world every Christmas.

Boring as these Sunday night suppers could be, it taught us the valuable lesson of making small talk and being polite when we didn't feel like it. I'm really good at small talk still, though I try not to have to practise it too often.

I was still determined to get into university to study drama. The only place to offer an undergraduate degree course was Bristol where it was notoriously difficult to get in. I knew that I was reasonably bright (if I worked hard), but I was certainly no genius and the Baby Boomers, born towards the end of the Second World War were about to apply for university places like never before. So, to have an alternative I applied for, and got, a place to study stage management at the Central School of Speech and Drama in London.

Then, towards the end of the spring term I got the exciting news that I had a conditional offer from Bristol University for the following autumn. I'd never even had an interview but Tabby must have given me good references – it had been worth all those dreary suppers. I was ecstatic, but still doubtful about my ability to get good enough marks, so, in the Easter holidays Mum and I went to London for my interview at the Central School.

Bizarre as it may seem today for a seventeen-year-old, I had never been to London before. It was a long way from the north and people just didn't travel very far afield. Mum, however, was determined to push the boat out on this trip. We stayed at the very understated, but very up-market Brown's Hotel. We took a taxi around the sights, had tea at Fortnum and Mason's and went to see My Fair Lady and Pieces of Eight, Kenneth Williams' first major review.

I was amazed at how adeptly my mum found her way around, but we never got lost, not even on our way to Hampstead on the tube for my interview. I really liked the school and they seemed happy to take me so, although Bristol was still my first choice, I felt very relaxed about where I would finally end up.

Back at school it was full steam ahead for the exams.

I honestly can't remember whether I found the papers hard or easy, all I wanted by then was for them to be over. I'd had more than enough of school by this time. My last exam was on my eighteenth birthday but we didn't have much in the way of a celebration since there were still three weeks of term to be endured. We mooned about playing tennis and swimming and making the odd trip into the town – I'd gone off knitting by this time – and then it was Speech Day, our very last one.

I won a lot of prizes. We all did in the upper sixth because by this time there were so few of us and several of the prizes were awarded for such things as being school prefects, as they were every year. The prize I was proudest of, of course, was the one for drama but I can't remember what the others were for even though I have them somewhere still.

Afterwards Mum and Rob took Wee Holy and me out to a very smart dinner which I think she really enjoyed. I realised, not for the first time, what genuinely nice people my parents were in the way they put this shy little lady at her ease. I enjoyed it too did but I shouldn't have tried to be grown up and have a liqueur at the end. It was an early lesson of Life.

After that it was all systems go for the last few days of term and, for some of us, the end of life as it had been for so long. The upper sixth had a pep talk from Tabby in which she advised us to be, ahem ...well, very careful in our dealings with young men and always to try to get to Holy Communion on Easter Sunday. I have largely kept to the last bit of advice.

Then we packed our trunks which were sent on in advance, cleared our desks, gathered up our treasures and said many fond and often tearful farewells before getting on the buses which were to take us to the station for the journey home. As we went over the little bridge at the bottom of the hill we threw our Panama hats in the river as a symbol of our new independence and got ready to celebrate the new and exciting life which so soon awaited us.

Ready to go out into the world, aged 18

Chapter 18

SALAD DAYS

I waited to hear if I had done well enough in my A levels to be accepted by Bristol. And waited. And waited.

At the end of my second holiday with the Manleys in Saundersfoot (on the Gower Peninsular), things got very serious and I spent a lot of time hanging about outside the local Post Office waiting for my results to arrive. They finally came on the postcard I had written to myself – no looking on line then – and I had passed all three. But had I done well enough to get into Bristol University? It would be another agonising month before I found out.

In the end Uncle Joey, who still seemed to be in charge of my education, rang the Registrar's office – he believed in starting at the top and, in any case, this was well before the foundation of UCAS.

He was told that I was top of the waiting list and in every previous year this would have guaranteed me a place vacated by someone who had had a better offer.

This year – the baby boomers had now grown up and were jostling for university –it simply wasn't happening but they would let us know. This didn't sound at all promising and, as I already had an unconditional place at the Central School of Speech and Drama in London, I decided to take it.

And so it was that one bright September day in 1960, Mum, Rob and I set off on the train for London Town. They had booked in at a hotel (Brown's, I expect) and I had found 'digs', as student lodgings used to be called, with one Mrs Dalrymple in smart Lexham Gardens, Kensington, where I shared a room with an old schoolfriend of mine, Caromy Jenkins.

Mrs Dalrymple was a real snob and she was pretty doubtful about me on account of coming from 'the North'. Caromy was a northern girl too but I expect Mrs Dalrymple 'knew' her family. I certainly wasn't one of her usual lodgers who were girls studying at secretarial colleges and meeting their boyfriends at the Cavalry Club on Saturday mornings.

Dear, patient Mum and Rob spent the weekend practising the journey with me between Kensington and Swiss Cottage, Hampstead, where the Central School was. Backwards and forwards we went until I knew almost every inch of the way, and then they set off back home on the train.

This was the first time I was actually grateful for those awful days at boarding school because, although I missed them, I wasn't actually at all homesick. It was all too exciting.

The first morning I turned up at the Central School in a great state of excitement. This was where so many of the great names of the theatre had trained and, although I was studying stage management and not acting, I was actually HERE.

And I loved it from the minute I stepped through the door and made lots of friends that first day. One of these was a boy called Derry Barber whose father hosted a famous radio quiz show and whose mother wrote a television drama. He insisted from then on, on collecting me from Lexham Gardens and coming with me to the school. So much for all the practise on the underground – we caught the bus.

I don't know if Mrs Dalrymple ever caught sight of Derry, in his shabby jeans and duffle coat, sitting on her elegant steps, waiting for me. She certainly never commented.

On the Thursday night I had a phone call from Mum. 'You've got a place at Bristol,' she said sounding pretty excited.

'I don't want it now, I'm just loving it here,' was my rather deflating reply.

'Meet me at Euston tomorrow at 6 o'clock,' she said. And, as I've mentioned before, you didn't argue with my mum.

On the Saturday morning we went to the college for an interview with Tubby Hayes who was running the course and he gave me some very sound advice. 'If you were my daughter I'd suggest that you went to university now and came back to us afterwards if you still want to go into the theatre.' I've never forgotten those words of wisdom.

Back to St Annes went Mum and me and two days later we were on the train to Bristol. Because I was such a late starter I hadn't been allocated a place in a hall of residence – thank goodness – I didn't to live with a lot of other people ever again or to have to stick to more rules and regulations. My new digs were with lovely Mrs McKee in Hampton Road in the Redland area of Bristol. I shared a room with one other girl – a rather eccentric medical student called Jan – and we also had a little sitting/dining room where Mrs McKee brought us delicious meals. I really felt I had fallen on my feet.

Next day Mum went home (poor Mum, however many miles had she travelled in the last ten days?) and I was left to sample the hurly-burly of Freshers' Week which was now in full swing with stalls representing every sort of society laid out in front of us and students begging us to join. Which to choose? It really was very confusing.

It was here that I got into conversation with a slim girl with dark wavy hair who told me her name was Sally and that she came from Staffordshire and had been to a school belonging to the same foundation as QE and where Tabby, my old headmistress had been educated. We became firm friends on that day and we have been friends ever since. For reasons which I can't now quite remember we called each other Ada and we are still Ada to this day.

I'll always remember that first term as a time of enormous delight. Ada and I took part in whatever was going – I played a prostitute in a one act play and danced in a chorus line in black fishnet tights. We spent hours in the Berkeley, the café across the road from the university building, with a group of our friends, putting the world to rights and smoking the products of W D & H O Wills, the founders of the university, before their lethal contents had been analysed. A packet of ten was usually empty when it had been passed round but so far as I know the drug scene was not then a part of student life.

We met in pubs or basement coffee bars in the evening or in the students' union bar in the imposing Georgian

Victoria Rooms. We did the minimum of work because we were too busy enjoying ourselves but some had to be done because the threat of being sent down for failing first part finals at the end of the year hung over us.

Anyway, I enjoyed what I was doing. Drama was a new university subject and we felt privileged to be part of it. All the people who taught us had written the definitive book on their subject. Most prominent of these was Professor Glyn Wickham whose appointment several years before had made him the youngest professor in the country. He wasn't a brilliant lecturer but his book, Early English Stages, the history of the theatre in the British Isles, was a must and he was, as Ada and I were later to find out, a particularly nice man.

He always seemed somewhat distant, unlike Marian Jones who was very keen to fraternise with the students on our terms. 'Call me Marian, ducky,' was her catch phrase, but Ada and I never did because it didn't seem right for us all to be on equal terms. She was Miss Jones to us and Miss Jones she remained.

One of our English lecturers was the poet A C Tomlinson whose work was well known then. He was not good at lecturing in a crowded hall but his tutorials were magical and I was lucky enough to have him as my tutor. Our main history lecturer was a Churchillian character whose name now escapes me but his lectures on early history were never to be forgotten, delivered in dramatic tones as he marched about, his gown flowing behind him. It was all a great change from our schoolteachers.

But by far the most eccentric was John Steer who lectured in history of European art, a subject which Ada and I took just for a year and which we really loved. We still go to art exhibitions together even now. Mr Steer used to drift around the university as though he was in a dream and he probably was. He was appointed to be our moral tutor and we weren't quite sure how much help he was going to give us if we needed it but he was very helpful and supportive when Granny was seriously ill just before I took my first part finals. We came to like him a lot.

Although I did the minimum of work – there wasn't time for more – I realised that, not being the brightest student it was a good idea to go to as many lectures as possible and take a lot of notes. And as I had a very good memory I was able to get by. But we all had a nasty surprise at the end of our first term when most of us failed our drama exam. Shock horror! I had never not done well in exams since the dreaded maths.

It was a wake up call and from then on I did pay a bit more attention to work, but not much less to enjoyment.

To girls from a single sex boarding school it was boys that were the main attraction. The ratio in those day was four boys to every girl and fresher girls were particularly popular. Although I dearly loved Johnny, the boy I had left at home, I wasn't going live in purdah in the term time. Ada and I had lots of dates, mostly to gigs, films or – and this was a dodgy one – to 'come to my rooms for tea'. In my innocence I thought that was what they meant and I quickly developed various escape strategies when I found that it wasn't.

By the end of the first term we had both had several boyfriends but Ada then started going out seriously with a boy called Alastair to whom she later became engaged while I went home to the lovely Johnny who was struggling to pass maths O level in order to get into Cambridge. He must have found me a real pain because I couldn't stop talking about what a good time I was having. Before I left in the Autumn I had introduced him to Martin and they are still good friends today.

I went home to spend Christmas in the bosom of my loving family and I loved it but, somehow, things had changed. I was used to pleasing myself not to being in by a certain time at night, and to going out and doing as I pleased without asking anyone if it was all right.

But we had a lovely Christmas and it was good to see all my friends, especially Johnny, again. On New Year's

Eve we went to the dinner dance at the Royal Lytham and St Annes Golf Club, a venerable institution on a par with the Royal and Ancient Golf Club at St Andrew's – or so its members thought.

New Year's Eve was the only time Mum would go to Royal Lytham because on all other occasions women had to go in by a separate entrance through a smelly locker room. Mum wasn't a rabid feminist but she had her principals and she passed them on to me. Rob just didn't get it and it caused about the only arguments he and I ever had. They went on to the end of his life. 'But it's always been like that,' he protested.

In truth, I was itching to get back to Bristol and the life I was loving so much. Ada moved into Mrs McKee's with me and Jan went off to share with a medical student friend. We had a lot of fun and I think Mrs McKee enjoyed it too and often joined in our discussions. Our friends really envied our digs and a lot of them often crowded into our tiny sitting room for endless cups of coffee.

Rag Week was traditionally the first week in March and the first time was particularly exciting. The students dressed up in even more weird clothes and did mad things to raise money for charity. A lot of us went out collecting money – we were assigned to a particularly poor area of the city and I remember being very touched by how generous people were.

Ada and I got caught up in a real live and very frightening riot in the city centre where a boxing ring had been set up. As people were fighting in there the crowd threw in money and on this occasion a soldier from the local barracks and a sailor whose boat had recently docked in Bristol got up to fight. It all got very noisy and suddenly Ada's boyfriend Ali said, 'Come on girls, we've got to get out,' and steered us through the crowd which was beginning to turn nasty. Police and police dogs appeared and eventually the crowd was dispersed but it wasn't a pleasant few minutes. The newspapers had a field day.

'Did you read about the riots and weren't you worried?' I asked when I phoned Mum the next day.

'Of course not. I knew you wouldn't be involved,' was her confident reply.

Just before Rag Week I had got talking to a boy I'd never spotted before, outside the library, and we went over to the Berkeley for a coffee. It turned out that he had been following me to the library and had finally plucked up the courage to speak to me.

I was rather flattered and as we were getting on so well, I accepted his invitation to go to his closest friend's 21st birthday party the following Saturday. 'It's at another friend's house up on the Downs. His mother's away and she says we can do as we like as long as no one's sick on the carpet.'

Brave, or innocent, lady. I don't think anyone was sick but it was touch and go.

Brian (I did discover his name before I went out with him) came to collect me from Mrs McKee's) and off we went to John Hazell's party. John was wandering around with a bottle of gin in his hand and nobody seemed entirely sober. Brian explained that most of them had been up all the previous night at the 24 hour peddle car race which took place on Bristol's College Green as a Rag Week stunt and money raiser. They looked as though they had done a fair amount of celebrating since.

By the end of the evening it was obvious that Brian was quite incapable of taking me home so John took me instead and, good friend that he was, persuaded Brian to come round to apologise the next day. John, who had been both to prep school and public school with Brian, is still a good friend to both of us and so is his wife, Felicity.

What I couldn't guess at the time, was that in Brian I had met the man I was going to marry.

Rob, Martin, Mum and Brian with our
cat called Henry Bathurst

Chapter 19

MORE SALAD DAYS

When I went home for Easter, Brian and I wrote to each other every day and he also sent me poetry he had written. It was all very romantic.

I had to tell Johnny that I had met someone else who I felt serious about, and he was very nice about it – he was always nice – and we are still friends 60 years later.

I worked hard while I was at home because I was determined to pass my first part finals at the end of the year. Being sent down was not part of my plan. Brian, as far as I could tell, had done very little work all the time he had been a student and he was about to take his finals. When I got back I told him I had to work a lot in the next few weeks and he'd better do the same. He said it was one of the only reasons he managed to pass his finals.

Then Mrs McKee dropped a bombshell. Her husband had gone bankrupt and the house had to go on the market immediately. Ada and I were homeless at an incredibly important time. Mum came down again to help us find somewhere else to live – I think she was afraid we would spend the rest of the term dossing on other people's floors, and she wasn't far wrong.

Luckily for us all, Cousin Mary (Johnson) had just come to work at a very smart fashion shop in Park Street, Clifton, the posh area of Bristol, quite close to the university. Mum went to see her and discovered that she was staying at the YWCA (Young Women's Christian Association) hostel while she looked for somewhere for all the family to live when they came down from Yorkshire. Before we knew it Ada and I were booked in.

The YWCA was really awful – just like being back at school and we had to be in by 11 pm every night. But Mum, as ever, was right. We did need somewhere 'proper' to live for the next few weeks and we had a lot of laughs, mostly with Mary, and mainly about the warden Mrs Muller (yes, really), who we called the Frau.

But saying goodbye to Mrs McKee, who had been like a surrogate mother to us, was very sad, although we did visit her in nearby Clevedon where she and her family had gone to live.

The exams came and went and Ada and I passed quite easily. Brian scraped through and wasn't the flavour of the month with his father who had two first class honours degrees. But he had secured a job in Gloucester for the Autumn, so we could continue to see each other fairly often. Meanwhile Ada and I couldn't get out of 'the Y' quickly enough and we slept in a variety of places during the next few weeks. I ended up staying with Mary who had found a new home for the family and had been joined by my cousin Philip – we had a lot of fun.

We spent two weeks making a film as part of our drama course. It eventually lasted 20 minutes, was based on the Punch and Judy story and involved a vintage fire engine and a vintage white Rolls Royce. It took place in the grounds of Dyrham Park, a stately home not far from Bristol. The director was one of our lecturers, George Brandt, who was a small, plump and rather excitable man who kept jumping up and down and landing in cow pats.

'Watch out Mr Brandt!' someone would shout as he headed for another but it was always too late.

'Oh, s***!' he would say, every time it happened and who could contradict him? I was assistant wardrobe mistress and spent most of my time cleaning up the costumes, not often with great success.

But it was a lot of fun and Brian got in on the act too. We went out to Dyrham each day in a collection of clapped out old vehicles which were constantly breaking down. The drama lot had no idea about engines but Brian had and, he, as chief (and only) mechanic, proved to be one of the most popular members of the team.

In the meantime I had been to meet Brian's parents, who were very different from mine. They had been in India before the British were chucked out in 1947. Brian's mother had always lived in India and bitterly regretted having to move to damp, cold post war England. Looking back, I can't blame her but I didn't have much sympathy at the time. His father and I got on quite well together because I was studying history and English which were his particular subjects in which neither of his children were remotely interested. I think they quite liked me, although like Mrs Dalrymple they were suspicious of people from the North.

Before I went home for the holidays Brian asked me to marry him. I accepted and rang home excitedly to tell my parents. They were horrified, not because they didn't like Brian but I was only 19 and I think that, deep down, they still hoped that I would marry a boy from home. It just wasn't going to happen.

Ada and I had managed to find a sort of flat before we left Bristol for the holidays. It was in smart, but crumbling Victoria Square in the heart of Clifton and it was right at the top of a large Georgian house. We each had a room and the use of the kitchen and bathroom but our landlady, Mrs Lawrence, also lived there with her boyfriend Maurice, who we really didn't like much. But she was pretty lenient and I think she quite liked having us around. My room was right up in the roof and through the tiny, gabled window I could look out over the rooves of Bristol. I loved it.

But before I went back to Bristol, tragedy struck our family. Never robust, Granny had been very frail for some time and for the last few months she had been in a nursing home. For some time Mum and Uncle Joey had taken turns to sit with her day and most of the night and, of course, they were the most devastated when she died. Grandpa, old softy that he was, wept for his lost love – they must have been married for close on sixty years – but next to them, I was the closest to her because she had played such a big part in my childhood. She was always there for me, never taking sides (which I would really like her to have done) against my Mum's ruling but always making me feel that I had an ally, always listening to my hopes and dreams and encouraging me in most of the things I wanted to do. She wasn't just my granny, she was another mum.

I remember going for a walk with Rob when he told me that Granny couldn't have survived because in the end she had developed cancer and was too old and too frail for treatment. I was upset that I had been kept in the dark about this because I considered myself quite old enough to be told and, of course, I was.

But cancer was something that wasn't talked about then. Treatment was in its infancy and it was always assumed that it was a death sentence, which it usually was. But, as ever, I was grateful to Rob for telling me and it brought us even closer together.

It was the first funeral Hilary, Martin and I had been to and I can't remember much about it except that it was at St Cuthbert's Church at Lytham, which looked out over the Green and the sea, where Grandpa still sang in the choir and where our family have such long associations. She was buried in the same grave as her elder sister who had brought her up and where Grandpa would later join her. At the tea which followed we drank from Granny's dainty willow pattern cups which I still have, and I remember thinking, 'Is this how it all ends, with a cup of tea and a piece of cake?' But of course, it doesn't. Those whom you love never really die and I often think of Granny and how much she meant to me.

But I had my whole life in front of me and it was very exciting. I didn't forget Granny – I've never forgotten her – but it was time for me to go back to Bristol and immerse myself once more in my new life.

It was a bit strange without Brian and all his friends, who had become my friends, but I saw quite a lot of him as his parents had bought him a Mini for his birthday, which meant that he came back to Bristol at weekends. Also, several of them now worked for the Bristol Aircraft Company and shared a rather sordid flat in Cotham, in slightly downmarket Bristol. Most weekends there was a party there – it was the ideal place, there was certainly nothing there to spoil – and they had a policeman friend called Norman who came to warn us if we were making too much noise.

Looking back, it was all very innocent. The girls drank wine and the boys drank beer, drugs had not yet become a part of student life and the lack of any really effective contraceptive made sex a dodgy business.

My mother, however, had provided me with a fail-safe antidote in those days when illegitimacy was simply not acceptable and abortion was illegal. 'If you ever get pregnant without a husband, I shall walk into the sea till my hat floats,' she had said to me.

She always did what she said she would do, and although this seemed a bit extreme, I couldn't take the risk. The trouble was, I knew where she would do it. There was a place called Granny's Bay between Lytham and St Annes which was a favourite spot for would-be suicides. The picture of her hat (though she seldom wore one) floating out sea spoiled many a romantic moment.

I missed the old bustle of 'the boys' (Brian and his friends), but I met someone who turned out to be a friend for life. When we got back to Bristol, Ada introduced me to Heather who had been a friend of hers at school. She was an incredibly pretty girl who I thought at first was rather shy while she thought I was a bit frosty. How we laughed when we confessed this to one another. Heather was the least shy person I ever knew and she admitted that I was one of the friendliest. She and I became close friends for the rest of our lives.

Heather didn't have a very happy home life as her parents were rather snobbish and had clear ideas of the sort of man she should marry. She met her future husband, Mike, as a result of meeting one of his friends at our wedding. But her parents did not approve, mainly because he didn't come from Bolton where they lived and, horror of horrors, he had left university without completing his degree.

He was the loveliest man she could ever have met and we supported them all the way. Finally Heather left home one winter night, taking very little with her, and she and Mike came to stay with us in our rather cramped flat before they went to Mike's family in Devon.

When they married, Brian gave Heather away and she wore my wedding dress. Mike returned to university and eventually set up a very successful business selling his own inventions worldwide and employing over 70 people. They had three lovely sons and lived in a beautiful Devon stone farmhouse converted largely by Mike and the boys, where Heather ran a very successful farmhouse holiday business until Mike was properly set up.

How mistaken her parents were.

Heather joined the little gang of us who called ourselves the Adas. The other two Adas were engineers called Mike and Dick and we had lunch together every day in the university refectory. The food wasn't great but it was very cheap and as Ada, Heather and I were all used to boarding school food and the two boys came from rather poor homes where the food was never lavish, it suited us fine.

Something I realised very quickly was that us girls came from a privileged middle class background and a lot of our friends didn't. It was a very useful lesson to learn. It hadn't always been so at the seats of academic learning since it was only recently that bright kids from working class families could come to university on grants. Also, we met other students of all creeds and colours from lands which so far we had only read about in books.

Abdul and Ali, for instance, were the sons of Somali sheiks and Seneca was the nephew of Mrs Banderonike, the first woman prime minister of Sri Lanka, then called

Ceylon. Their countries have suffered terribly through war and revolution and I often wonder what happened to them. These overseas students were always wealthy and predominantly male – they came from a man's world where there were no educational grants.

We had a lot of fun and a lot of laughs that year when the pressure of exams had subsided for the time being, though we did have end of the year exams which I suppose we would have had to sit again if we had done really badly. I was determined to keep up with the workload, though, since I simply wasn't bright enough to pass exams of any sort without working hard for them.

I found that going to lectures and writing copious notes saved endless time looking for facts in the library. But Ada and I had come to the same conclusion about our theatrical careers. We had neither the talent nor the enthusiasm to be successful in the professional theatre. We just had to concentrate on getting reasonable degrees and find a good job when we graduated.

It wasn't going to be easy – interesting careers for girls, even if they were graduates, were very hard to come by in the 1960s.

Sand yaghting, which briefly took
over from riding

Chapter 20

TAKING LIFE SERIOUSLY

Third year students all over the country returned to university determined to take life seriously. Our Salad Days were over and it was down to work. Or was it? Nothing really felt very urgent, in fact nothing really had changed and finals, after all, weren't until next June. There was plenty of time and besides, two years as students had shown us how to cut corners. We went back to discussing Life Itself in smoky coffee bars, keeping the pubs going with our custom and going to gigs on Saturday nights.

Things had changed a bit in our living arrangements though, as Ada had decided to live in a flat in Bristol's magnificent but crumbling Royal York Crescent. I stayed with Mrs Lawrence as I loved my little skylight room, and the girl who replied to my advert for someone else to rent the other room, also became a friend for life.

Sue was very funny. She was also very attractive and very clever – she was studying German, and planned to join the British Council when we graduated. She had spent a rather quiet two years sharing digs with a very studious girl called Ann Tait, and I think Sue enjoyed all the people who called for coffee and a smoke at Mrs Lawrence's. She later travelled the world but we always kept in touch and we still do, and also with Ann who lives near me, in Cheltenham.

Luckily for me, given all these distractions, the subjects I was by then studying – drama, English and history – required a lot of work to be presented during the term, and I wrote a detailed essay once a week as well as going to all the lectures and tutorials. I wasn't being a swot, I simply wasn't clever enough to bluff my way to that precious degree without putting in some spadework. Besides, although Mum, Rob and Daddy all told me that as long as I did my best they would be happy, that wasn't good enough for me. I had to pass those exams with honours or I would not forgive myself.

I can't remember whether it was Uncle Joey or Auntie Stella who once said to my parents, 'Of course, it's all right for Di – she's clever.'

Secretly, I was fuming. It just wasn't true – I had to put in the hours. I knew many students at Bristol who didn't have to do much work because they really were clever. Alan Dosser, for example, would sit in an exam for a short time, usually eating something, leave the exam room and get excellent results. He went on to be director of the Everyman Theatre in Liverpool and merited a long obituary in both The Times and The Telegraph when he died (I don't know how flattered he would have been by this, the only newspaper I remember him reading was The Daily Worker).

Luckily for me, I had a very good memory (in those days) and if I read and re-read the notes I had laboriously scribbled in lectures, I could usually do reasonably well, but never brilliantly.

But before we could get too worked up about exams, two completely different things happened, one of which could have scuppered everybody's future, not just ours. This was the Cuban Missile Crisis of October 1962.

Just as the fear of climate change now hangs over the whole of society, then it was the fear of nuclear extinction. Since the Americans had dropped the first atom bombs on Hiroshima and Nagasaki in 1945 there was a great dread of a similar disaster happening again, only this time it would be the much more powerful hydrogen bomb which could wipe vast tracts of land and millions of people – or so we thought.

Nobody really knew and that made it even more scary. The two main powers with nuclear bombs were the USA in the west and the USSR (Russia) in the east, both with totally opposing ideologies. Lurking behind the threat was Nikita Kruschev, who had come to power after the death of Stalin. He was determined to establish nuclear weapons within range of the USA. And he didn't do things by halves.

That fateful October, the USA discovered that Cuba was building missile launch sites that were capable of launching Russian nuclear weapons. Worse still, it seemed that Russian ships were bringing further weapons. The idea of Russian nuclear weapons being sited so close to American soil was a terror which US President John F Kennedy dared not tolerate.

Kennedy sent a message to the Soviet leader Kruschev demanding that the existing launching sites were dismantled and his ships turned back. Kruschev refused. For a fearsomely tense few days the world stood on the brink of a nuclear war.

Then, finally, both sides agreed to a deal that diffused the tension. We all breathed again.

Grandpa always used to say that he remembered exactly where he was at times of historical crisis and I certainly know where I was when the Cuban Missile Crisis happened.

I had gone to spend the evening with Brian who rented a little flat in a farmhouse near Standish, a village not far from Gloucester, where he worked.

We sat together, holding hands and not speaking as we listened on the radio to the crisis unfolding. We had no idea what the result would be but we thought of all the plans we had made for the future. Would there be a future for any of us? Everything was still uncertain as he took me back to Bristol later that evening in the little red Mini. It had no radio so we didn't know what was happening and it wasn't until the next morning that we heard how the crisis had been defused.

Phew …

The second event that impacted upon my preparation for my exams came from a sharp turn in the weather. It began when Brian and I spent the Christmas with his parents in Kent. It was the first Christmas that I hadn't been at home and I was miserable. The Alexanders were not a Christian family and it was the first time that I hadn't been to church on Christmas morning since I was a toddler. It was just a day of present giving, drinking and eating.

Luckily, after a visit to Great Aunt Lil who I loved, we went to spend Christmas Day with Brian's sister, also Diana, and her husband Ernest. Also joining us were most of Ernest's family – and there were a lot of them, all very cheerful cockneys from London's docklands. They were really good fun and I made particular friends with

Ernest's Mum and his sister Edie with whom I always exchanged Christmas cards. They didn't mind that I came from Lancashire …

We woke up on Boxing Day to leaden skies and a few snowflakes floating about. We had intended to stay until the next day and then drive north to my family but as we watched the snowflakes come down faster and faster, Brian, always a man of action, said, 'We need to go now.'

We packed our things, including our presents, and set off for the north.

It was some journey. Snow fell all the time and at first we couldn't get any petrol because the pump mechanisms had frozen. Finally we managed to fill up and off we went again. Thank goodness for the Mini – she kept moving on the slippery roads, when others were stuck. After what seemed like hours, and probably was (no motorways then – only the Preston by-pass right at the end), we arrived. There was even a light covering of snow in St Annes, which showed how severe it was because that hardly ever happened.

Mum and Rob were delighted to see us but I don't think they'd been very worried because they had no idea how bad it was away from the coast.

On New Year's Eve Brian was treated to the sight of my Mum and me, dressed to the nines, swanning into the Golf Club through the main entrance. Rob still didn't get why we were so triumphant. That was in the early 60s. I heard from Martin not very long ago that everyone could now come and go by the main entrance but that the women members were now complaining because they had to pay an annual fee equal to that of the men. There's no pleasing some people.

Brian was a bit of a cause celebre at the Golf Club. Everybody wanted to meet 'Diana's young man', which I think he, being rather shy, found a bit overwhelming.

He was given plenty of advice about his journey home – 'take a shovel,' 'make sure you have a blanket, a hot drink, Wellington boots etc.' All kindly meant, but what did they know of real weather, safe in their little seaside sanctuary? What did we know either, come to that? But we were shortly to find out.

People still talk in hushed tones about the severity of the winter of 1962–3. The snow and ice lasted for three months. It seemed set to go on forever.

When I returned to Bristol after Christmas, I found icy streets and frozen pipes. We had no tap water at Mrs Lawrence's for most of the term – there was a standpipe on the pavement from which we could get water, which then had to be carried up three flights of stairs – four in my case – and an Elsan chemical closet instead of the lavatory. Suddenly Maurice, Mrs L's boyfriend who we all disliked, became extremely popular because it was he who had to carry the Elsan down the stairs to empty it into the tank which took the contents away.

Sue and I, joined by Ada, used to steal the occasional bath at Clifton Hill House, the hall of residence where Heather lived, with Heather on guard in case the warden appeared – it was larks in the dorm all over again. Otherwise we kept a toothbrush and a face flannel with us at all times and washed in the university cloakrooms, along with a lot of other students in the same position as us.

I went to bed in as many layers of clothing as I could find, including several pairs of socks and my most unattractive winceyette pyjamas last worn at school, with a hot water bottle which cooled off very quickly. The water in the glass by my bed would be frozen the next morning. That was the penalty for living so near the roof…Perhaps for the first time Ada, Heather and I were thankful for our boarding school years. They had taught us to be ready for most emergencies.

Brian just managed to get to work each morning and we would spend the weekends walking along the tops of drystone Cotswold walls (the footpaths were deeply buried), looking out over a white wilderness. We little thought that this was what we would be doing during snowy spells for many years to come.

As far as our studies were concerned, dealing first with the threat of nuclear war and then an impossible winter seemed to take the urgency out of working for our finals. We all seemed to feel that there would be plenty of time when things returned to normal. We were cutting it pretty fine. Then Ada and I had an enormous stroke of luck.

I was in the drama department one afternoon when Lesley, Professor Wickham's secretary, was coming along the corridor asking if anyone could babysit for the Professor's children – that night. Without a second thought I said, 'I'll go. And can I take Sally Robinson (Ada's official name) with me?'

Lesley looked incredibly relieved and it was all fixed up.

We turned up that chilly February evening to a large Georgian house in upmarket Clifton where we were met by a very relieved looking Mrs Wickham who showed us round the house and introduced us to the three children, Stephen, Catherine and Christopher. It's worth noting here that neither Ada nor I, both being only children, had never had many dealings with small people.

Perhaps it was an advantage – it must have been because we all immediately got on together and from then on they demanded that Sally and Di should look after them when their parents went out. We told them endless stories, mainly simplified tales from Shakespeare – it seemed a good idea since their father was a Shakespearian scholar – but what they enjoyed best were tales of horror about a ghastly creature called The Fang. How we got the idea for that, I can't now remember.

To volunteer for babysitting was quite without motive at the time but we soon realised that to be friendly with the Wickham family would not do us any harm academically. Besides we really loved those children and they loved us. So much so, that when Ada and I arrived slightly late for a party at the Wickham's after our exams were all over, there was a commotion on the landing and three little pyjama-clad figures rushed down the stairs and threw themselves into our arms. 'Where have you been? We've been waiting for you for ages! Mummy and Daddy said we could stay up till you came.'

Imagine the scene in the Wickham's hall. All the students and dons were sipping their wine and talking about lofty things like symbolism (which I never really understood) and the merits of Beckett over Pinter or vice versa when their earnest discussions were interrupted by this commotion. We hadn't made names for ourselves with our dramatic or academic prowess, yet here we were, being treated like part of the Wickham family. It was a sweet moment – the more so for being completely unrehearsed – we weren't much into rehearsing.

Roll on four decades and Ada and I arrived at the celebration of 50 years of the Drama Department, now in a very state of the art building. Having been largely ignored by George Brandt because we weren't making films, the next person we saw was Mrs Wickham. 'Sally and Di!' she exclaimed, 'You must come and meet the children.'

The children by now were in their forties but they hadn't forgotten us.

'We never forgot those stories about The Fang', said Catherine, giving us both a hug. We had never forgotten the children either and our time spent with them ranked with some of the best of our salad days.

But back to the looming exams and I decided I'd probably get more done if I went home, out of the way of distractions. Anyway, I was getting tired of the Elsan closet and the stand pipe in the road. I looked forward to Mum's cooking and a hot bath when I felt like it. And I did work hard - but would it be hard enough? I returned to Bristol full of trepidation.

Once they had begun the exams weren't too bad and I reckoned I'd done well enough to get the coveted honours degree. The results were published on the university main notice board on June 24 – my 21st birthday. They weren't put up until the afternoon and we spent the time in the pub across the road, taking it in turns to go and see if they were there. What a way to spend that particular milestone in my life.

Ada and I both got a 2:2 degree, Sue got a 2:1 and so did Dosser which we had expected. Today a 2:2 wouldn't be considered to be much but in those days when first class honours were seldom awarded (though Ann Tait fulfilled her ambition) we were very pleased. We spent the next week celebrating – both the exam results and my birthday – it was one long party.

Graduation took place before we went home, not months later as happens today. I bought a new dress for the graduation ball, Brian joined us and we all danced the night away, though we were somewhat subdued by the feeling that it was nearly the end of this golden time of our lives.

Mum, Rob and Step-Granny came down for the ceremony – for Step-Granny it was very nostalgic to return to the city where she had trained to be a teacher nearly sixty years ago.

In our hired gowns and mortar boards we waited in the Colston Hall with hundreds of other students until finally it was our turn to step onto the stage and receive our degrees from, I think, the Vice-Chancellor, Sir Philip Morris, though now a lot of that day is a bit of a blur.

But it didn't matter – we had done what we set out to do during a time that none of us would ever forget.

The graduate at last

On the swing that Daddy made

Chapter 22

THE VERY END

My account of being a kid wouldn't sound good to child psychologists today. I didn't see my father till I was three, my parents divorced and I was thirteen when I met him again. My mother remarried and then I was packed off to boarding school which I hated. Surely I must have been traumatised? But I really wasn't because I always knew I was loved both by my family and my friends. I loved them in return, unreservedly, and they knew it.

Being an 'only child' is often thought to be synonymous with 'spoiled brat', but I have seldom found this to be true. If you have no siblings you desperately need friends and you don't make them by being spoiled and selfish. Besides, in my case, my Mum wouldn't have stood for it …

The friends I made when I was a kid and then a student are still my friends today – we are godparents to each others' children, we meet as often as we can, and we share our joys and sorrows. They have enriched my life, and I'd like to think that, in a small way, I have enriched theirs.

Postscript

TO WORK

Before we took our final exams, all third year students had a meeting at the Appointments Board where we were given advice on what our job options were. It never occurred to us at the time that there was a difference between the options presented to the male or female students.

For the boys there were several companies all waiting to employ them, but for the girls it was a very different matter. Those women who had studied such career subjects as medicine or the law (there were very few female engineers in those days) would be pretty certain about what the future would hold, but for the rest of us there were very few options.

A job – any job – in the theatre had been our original ambition but by this time it was obvious that wasn't going to happen. The BBC was another 'choice' but you had to know someone who could get you an interview, and even then most of the jobs involved making tea until a lucky break came your way. Most of us were told that for a female arts graduate, teaching was the only option.

This was pretty deflating after all our hard work and the kudos of getting into university at all, which was still pretty novel in those days. Having got myself a place to study for a Dip Ed (Diploma of Education) as it was then called, in Bristol, I had a long discussion with myself and decided that I wasn't going to take the so-called only choice available.

Besides, Brian and I were due to get married that autumn and I really didn't fancy travelling every day to Bristol from Cheltenham, where we were going to live. I cancelled my place and enrolled at the Phyllis Christie Secretarial College in Cheltenham the following January. I absolutely hated it – it was worse than being back at school except I didn't live at the college like most of the girls – and I was absolutely hopeless at typing, though shorthand was OK.

But I have never, never regretted it because it was an introduction to my first job with a public relations company (I had no idea what public relations was), which led eventually to my becoming a journalist.

There I found that a female graduate with a secretarial qualification was very employable, and I began my lifelong career. So much for the Appointments Board.

CHOOSING MY
WEDDING DRESS

Even though we were now 'grown up', Hilary and I, together with my Mum and Auntie Stella, could seldom keep straight faces when we were out together, especially when engaged on a serious mission.

This particular mission, in the August after I left Bristol, occurred when Mum decided it was time we went to look for a wedding dress for me and a bridesmaid's dress for Hilary. Forsaking the local department stores, we set off for Manchester and Kendall Milnes, then known as the Harrod's of the north. Mum had decided to start from the top. I'm not sure how good an idea it was.

Luckily Mum was driving since Auntie Stella, by her own admission, was an erratic driver. The story of her first descent from a multi-storey car park, when she lost control of the car and crashed into the barrier at the bottom, is still related in the family today.

I really liked the first dress I tried on. It was cream silk with little sprays of flowers woven into the material and it was a very flattering design with a large bow at the back and a train that was part of the dress. But it seemed a bit unadventurous to choose the first one I tried on so I struggled into a few more that the assistant had selected and still couldn't decide.

We had lunch at Kendall's and then set out to find other wedding dress shops in Manchester. The last dress I tried on in the fifth shop had a collar like an Elizabethan ruff. As my head shot through it, I felt (and looked) like Toby dog in a Punch and Judy show.

I was overcome by an uncontrollable fit of giggles and one by one, the others joined in. The shop assistant was mystified and we were laughing too much even to speak. I parted company with the dress as quickly as I could and we had to leave without explanation.

'So what are we going to do now?' Mum asked me as soon as she was able.

'Actually,' I confessed, 'I really liked that first dress I tried on.'

No one was grumpy with me because that had been their favourite too and, in any case, we were all keen to get home and we didn't want to go empty handed. Hilary admitted that she had loved the deep red bridesmaid's dress that she had first tried on too. Back we went to Kendall's. We had the dresses packed up and went home still giggling but feeling very satisfied with our purchases.

Both dresses were a great success and mine was worn

twice more, once by my dear friend Heather who I had met at Bristol, and again by Emily, my youngest daughter. It's still hanging in our loft because I can't bring myself to part with it.

THE FINAL HOLIDAY

We were heading for Scotland – Mum, Rob, Martin and I – for what we knew was to be our final family holiday. I was getting married in two months' time and Martin was off to college – it was the end of an era.

Our destination was a tiny hamlet called Portsonachon on the banks of Loch Awre. We'd been there before so we knew how much we'd enjoy it but this holiday was memorable for a different reason.

The Hotel Portsonachon was run by a delightful couple, Colonel and Mrs Young, and people mainly went there for the fishing – and the food, for Mrs Young's cuisine was to die for. It wasn't as gargantuan as Mrs Johnson's at Hodge Hill but this was all to the good: Mum and I didn't want to get home to find that we could no longer get into our wedding outfits.

Every morning and evening Colonel Young, wearing his kilt, walked round the outside of the hotel playing the bagpipes. Although we knew that this was really a bit of a gimmick to impress the American visitors, it was rather lovely to wake up to the sound of the pipes outside the window and in the evening, if we were out on the Loch, to row home to the strains of Scotland the Brave and The Scottish Soldier, echoing across the water.

We spent a lot of time on the Loch, not just for the fishing. Rob and Martin fished every day and Mrs Young cooked what they had caught – delicious. Mum and I had a different reason for our outings on the water. This was August 1963 when the events known collectively as the Profumo Scandal rocked Britain and particularly the British Government.

John Profumo was the Secretary for Defence in the Conservative government of Harold Macmillan and he had become involved with a very young and pretty showgirl called Christine Keeler whom he had met at a swimming party at Clivedon, the stately home of the Astor family. What turned the affair into a cause celebre was when it was discovered that Christine was also involved with a Russian diplomat named Yevgeny Ivanov who was suspected of being a spy.

Added to this mix was a very volatile jazz singer called Lucky Gordon and his dangerous rival Johnny

Edgecombe, who each believed he was Christine's boyfriend. The puppet master was a society osteopath named Stephen Ward who had many friends in high places, and owned the flat where Christine lived with another young woman, also a showgirl. Stephen Ward was put on trial for living off immoral earnings taken from the two young women, and the whole story connecting a senior government minister to a Russian spy came out. It was the stuff of a John le Carré novel, but this was real life ...

Profumo stood up in the House of Commons and denied the affair, which he later had to confess to. Ivanov was recalled to Moscow, and Stephen Ward was deserted by his influential friends and committed suicide – the scapegoat for the whole affair. Seldom had anything like this been reported in the British press before and they milked it for all it was worth.

The lounge at the Portsonachon Hotel was very quiet and genteel and Mum and I didn't feel comfortable reading about and discussing the trial in front of the other, rather elderly residents. So every morning we would drive to the nearest village, buy as many newspapers as we could find, collect the packed lunch we had ordered, and row down the Loch in one of the boats owned by the hotel.

There we would pull up the boat on a little beach we had found and spend the day reading and swapping newspapers. 'Have you seen this?', 'Wait till you read this bit,' and 'You'll never guess what she's said now,' were our only remarks until the papers were well and truly finished. Then we rowed back to the hotel, telling anyone who cared to ask what an interesting day we'd had.

In fact the whole affair was a dreadful tragedy for most of the people involved – Macmillan was a broken man and resigned as prime minister two months later, Profumo spent the rest of his life working with disadvantaged people in London's East End, Stephen Ward died unnecessarily and Christine Keeler never got the money she had hoped for by selling her story to the press. Christine's friend and flatmate, Mandy Rice-Davies came out of it the best. She married a rich man and led a relatively normal life.

Mum and I certainly didn't spend a normal holiday, but it was a memorable one.

Acknowledgements

My particular thanks to Lorna Brookes, my editor at Crumps Barn Studio for putting this book together so well, and my cousins Martin and Claire for supplying the photographs.